Ernest Sansbury

Seven Voices Around the Cross

and Other Sermons

by
Oliver B. Greene

The Gospel Hour, Inc., Oliver B. Greene, Director
Box 2024, Greenville, South Carolina 29602

First printing, September 1969—15,000 copies
Second printing, March 1970—15,000 copies

$5.00

FOREWORD

The Bible has much to do with *numbers*. We are not afforded time and space to go into this in detail in only one volume, but since *seven* is God's number for perfection we have chosen several instances involving that number.

Some of these sermons have appeared in our paper back publications, but it seems advantageous to publish them in one volume, which we send out with the hope and prayer that those who read this book will be inspired to "press toward the mark for the prize of the high calling of God in Christ Jesus."

The Author

CONTENTS

Foreword.. 3

Seven Voices Around the Cross......................... 9

Seven Words 43

Seven Things of God...................................... 107

Seven Pairs of Things 155

Seven Sets of Bible Twins 219

SEVEN VOICES AROUND THE CROSS

Seven Voices Around the Cross

"And they crucified Him, and parted His garments, casting lots: that it might be fulfilled which was spoken by the prophet, They parted my garments among them, and upon my vesture did they cast lots. And sitting down they watched Him there; and set up over His head His accusation written, THIS IS JESUS THE KING OF THE JEWS. Then were there two thieves crucified with Him, one on the right hand, and another on the left.

"And they that passed by reviled Him, wagging their heads, and saying, Thou that destroyest the temple, and buildest it in three days, save thyself. If thou be the Son of God, come down from the cross. Likewise also the chief priests mocking Him, with the scribes and elders, said, He saved others; Himself He cannot save. If He be the King of Israel, let Him now come down from the cross, and we will believe Him. He trusted in God; let Him deliver Him now, if He will have Him: for He said, I am the Son of God. The thieves also, which were crucified with Him, cast the same in His teeth.

"Now from the sixth hour there was darkness

9

over all the land unto the ninth hour. And about the ninth hour Jesus cried with a loud voice, saying, Eli, Eli, lama sabachthani? that is to say, My God, my God, why hast thou forsaken me? Some of them that stood there, when they heard that, said, This Man calleth for Elias. And straightway one of them ran, and took a sponge, and filled it with vinegar, and put it on a reed, and gave Him to drink. The rest said, Let be, let us see whether Elias will come to save Him.

"Jesus, when He had cried again with a loud voice, yielded up the ghost. And, behold, the veil of the temple was rent in twain from the top to the bottom; and the earth did quake, and the rocks rent; and the graves were opened, and many bodies of the saints which slept arose, and came out of the graves after His resurrection, and went into the holy city, and appeared unto many.

"Now when the centurion, and they that were with him, watching Jesus, saw the earthquake, and those things that were done, they feared greatly, saying, Truly this was the Son of God" (Matt. 27:35—54).

In these verses we have a record of six voices. Record of a seventh voice is found in another Gospel. At the outset let us realize that this is not a message on the seven sayings of Jesus. Many marvelous messages have been delivered and many wonderful books have been written on the seven sayings on the cross. *This* sermon does not have

10

to do with the seven sayings of Jesus, but with *seven voices* that were heard around the cross of Jesus. It has to do, not with words spoken by Jesus, but with words spoken to and about Jesus.

The Voice of Unholy Skepticism

The Scriptures tell us that they crucified Jesus, divided His garments, and gambled for His coat. All of this was a fulfillment of prophecy. They sat down, and watched Him—probably literally staring at the face of Jesus. Pilate had set up over His head the words, "This is Jesus, King of the Jews." On either side of Him a condemned thief was dying. Those who passed by the cross wagged their heads and said:

". . . *Thou that destroyest the temple, and buildest it in three days, save thyself. If thou be the Son of God, come down from the cross*" (Matt. 27:40). Here is the first recorded voice around the cross of Jesus. Let us call it "The voice of unholy skepticism." They were skeptics who cried out, "If thou be the Son of God, come down from the cross!"

Perhaps some of you are saying, "Don't you know those poor, pagan folks did not realize that the Man on the middle cross was an unusual man?" Is that what you are saying? Note this: these men were not stupid, nor were they heathen; they had watched Jesus from the very day He entered upon His public ministry. How do we know?

11

The first thing they shouted in His face shows that they had kept close check on Him. They said: "Thou that destroyest the temple and buildest it again in three days—save thyself!" Just when did Jesus utter the words referred to here?

Soon after He began His ministry, Jesus went into the temple, and found commercializers—money changers. They even had animals inside the temple. He chased these polluters out of God's house, turned over the money tables, and rebuked them. In the course of the message delivered at that time, Jesus said, "Destroy this temple, and in three days I will raise it up!" Those poor fellows thought He was referring to the beautiful temple in which they worshipped. They, like many today, could not rise above the natural; they could not receive the supernatural. They were students of prophecy—rulers, chief priests, elders, scribes, but they did not understand that Jesus was referring to His body:

"Then answered the Jews and said unto Him, What sign shewest thou unto us, seeing that thou doest these things? Jesus answered and said unto them, Destroy this temple, and in three days I will raise it up. Then said the Jews, Forty and six years was this temple in building, and wilt thou rear it up in three days? *But He spake of the temple of His body*" (John 2:18—21).

Note that the Pharisees sought a sign, and the Pharisees were the religious leaders of that day.

They opened the conversation by asking for a sign; and Jesus said, "Destroy this temple and I will raise it up in three days." They thundered back, "It took forty-six years to build it and you are going to raise it up in three days?" But Jesus was speaking of His body, not of the beautiful temple of which they were so proud.

Religion goes deep. It was firmly imbedded in the minds of these religionists. They had not forgotten the words of Jesus concerning what *they* thought was their beautiful temple, the beautiful house it took forty-six years to build. When they finally arrested Him and nailed Him to the cross, they hurled in His face the accusation, "That is the fellow! He is the One; look at Him! He said He would raise up the temple in three days, and He cannot even save Himself! If you are the Son of God, come on down; prove it by coming down from the cross!"

According to the teaching of Jesus, these men would not have believed had He stepped down from the cross. Why? Abraham said to the rich man in hell, "If your brothers do not believe Moses and the prophets, they would not believe one who rose from the dead!" (Luke 16:31). Religious skeptics have their minds made up. Skepticism and faith are as far apart as the North Pole is from the South Pole. These men had made up their minds. They demanded the death of Jesus; they hated Him in spite of His miracles—even *because* of His miracles—and they mocked Him while He died! They were unholy skeptics, and the words they spoke were the words of skeptics.

Dear reader, do you belong to the group represented by the *unholy skeptics?* Do you say, "I would be a Christian *if* . . . I would like to be saved *if.*" Many go on to say, *"If* I could be *sure* that I could live as a Christian ought to live, I would be saved." If . . . if . . . if . . . . Do you know who started the flow of "if's"? The devil did!

In Matthew 4, the devil said to the Lord Jesus, *"If* you are what you claim to be change these stones into bread." A second time the devil said, *"If* you are really the Son of God, go ahead and throw yourself down from the pinnacle of the temple; you will not be hurt—if you are who you claim to be." A third time the devil said to Jesus, *"If* you will worship me, I will give you, *free,* what you plan to die to redeem—all creation—man, the universe, all of God's creation that fell and was cursed because of Adam's sin." (Read Romans 8:32.) In other words, the devil said to Jesus, "Why don't you and I get together? Why not make a deal?" The devil knew that Jesus was to die, to bruise *his head.* Knowing that, he suggested that if they would get together, he would give to Jesus all the kingdoms of the earth.

There may be some who question that the kingdoms of the earth were the devil's to give; in case you doubt it, listen to this: "And the devil said unto Him, All this power will I give thee, and the glory of them: for that is delivered unto me; and to whomsoever I will I give it" (Luke 4:1—6).

There is entirely too much ignorance among believers concerning the power of the devil. According to the Word of God, he is the "prince of the power of the air" (Eph. 2:2). Jesus said, "Now is the judgment of this world: now shall the prince of this world be cast out" (John 12:31). Again, "Hereafter I will not talk much with you: for the prince of this world cometh, and hath nothing in me" (John 14:30). Again, "Of judgment, because the prince of this world is judged" (John 16:11). *Paul* tells us that the devil is the god of this world: "If our Gospel be hid, it is hid to them that are lost: in whom the *god of this world hath blinded the minds of them which believe not,* lest the light of the glorious Gospel of Christ, who is the image of God, should shine unto them" (II Cor. 4:3, 4).

The devil is a powerful being; none of us know just how powerful he is. "We wrestle not against flesh and blood, but against principalities, against powers, against the rulers of the darkness of this world, against spiritual wickedness in high places" (Eph. 6:12). Paul warns us to put on the whole armor of God that we may be able to stand against the wiles of the devil. No human being is a match for the devil. We overcome only because Christ lives in us (I John 4:4). If the devil tried to tempt *Jesus* to sell out, to worship and serve him, do you think he would hesitate to do his utmost to lead you and me to serve him?

Have you ever said, "If I knew that God is really God; if I knew there is really a heaven; if I knew there is really a hell; if I knew that a person can really be saved; if I knew salvation brings real joy; if I knew it was so simple as just believing on the Lord Jesus Christ and receiving Him, confessing with the mouth Jesus as Christ . . . if I knew it was that simple, I certainly would be saved!" Have you ever thought like this? Remember, it was the devil who raised the first question that appears in the Bible. That first question is: "Hath God said . . . ?" (Gen. 3:1). The devil is the originator of questions of doubt concerning God and His Word. Passers-by at the crucifixion shouted, *"If* you *are* the Son of God, come down from the cross!" Skeptics? Indeed they were! Beloved, do not be a skeptic. If God said it, God can do it! Everything in the Bible that pertains to man, especially the Jew and the nation Israel, has been and is being literally fulfilled before our eyes. Do not close your eyes to things that declare "There is a God!" Paul said to the Romans, "For the wrath of God is revealed from heaven against all ungodliness and unrighteousness of men, who hold the truth in unrighteousness; *because that which may be known of God* is manifest in them; for God hath shewed it unto them. For the invisible things of Him from the creation of the world are clearly seen, being understood by the things that are made, even His eternal power and Godhead; *so that they are without excuse"* (Rom. 1:18—20).

So when you look around you, when you gaze into the heavens, when you look upon the works of nature, let them speak to you of the reality of God. Surely no thinking person, after reading Matthew, Mark, Luke and John, would believe Jesus Christ, the Son of God, did not live on earth. He lived. Personally, I know He lived. He *lives* in my heart, and He wants to live in yours. Do not be a skeptic; be a believer!

The Voice of Unholy Preachers

We have the *second voice* speaking as recorded in Matthew 27:41, 42: "Likewise also the chief priests mocking Him, with the scribes and elders, said, *He saved others; Himself He cannot save. If He be the King of Israel, let Him now come down from the cross, and we will believe Him."* This is *the voice of unholy preachers,* who preached a gospel that will stand to condemn them in the day of judgment.

Truer words have never been uttered than the words "He saved others; Himself He cannot save!" If you believe the Word of God, you know Jesus did not come to save Himself; if He had saved Himself He could not have said, "It is finished."

If He had not accomplished the work the Father sent Him to do, then you and I would be destined to spend eternity in hell. Jesus could not save Himself. He was God in the flesh, He came to do the will of the Father, and the will of the Father was that Jesus lay down His life for the sins of the world (John 10:18). So these chief priests, scribes, and elders, authorities in religion in their day, preached the Gospel without realizing it.

These poor fellows had no conception of the mission of Jesus on earth. They were students of the Old Testament, they were leaders in religion, but they never understood the mission of the promised One. He came, not to save Himself, but to save *others*. He said, "I have come to seek and to save that which was lost." Again, "I came not to be ministered unto, *but to minister and to give my life a ransom for many.*" (See Luke 19:10 and Matthew 20:28.) If these unholy preachers had been *listening* when they attended the street meetings of Jesus, instead of watching His every move and listening to His every utterance to try to find some way to condemn Him, they would have known that He could not save Himself and still be able to fulfill His mission on earth, to finish the work the Father sent Him to do. In all of His sermons—whether in the house, in the temple, or on the street—He *made clear to His listeners* that He was in the world to do the will of His Father. The very fact that He saved others made it im-

18

possible for Him to save Himself!

These religious leaders were preaching the Gospel, they told the truth: He *could not* save Himself! They will face those words when they stand before the Great White Throne at the end of the ages, when God will judge by Jesus Christ, the Righteous Judge. They will distinctly *remember* (see Luke 16:25) the day they gazed upon Him as He hung upon the cross. They will distinctly remember their mocking words, "He saved others, Himself He cannot save. If He is King of Israel let Him prove it by coming down from that cross. If He will come down from the cross, we will believe Him." Jesus did not come into the world to come down from the cross; He came to *die* on the cross: "And I, if I be lifted up from the earth, will draw all men unto me" (John 12:32).

Since the devil has called, commissioned, and ordained ministers of his own (II Cor. 11:13—15) we have a perfect right to say these men were ministers of the devil, because they were working in co-operation with the devil, whether they realized it or not. The devil would have liked to see Jesus come down from the cross. The devil is not omnipotent or omniscient; but he did know that Jesus was the Seed that would bruise his head. He knew that if Jesus died on the cross, He had become a curse for all men; because it is written, "Cursed is everyone that hangeth on a tree." It was, therefore, through the spirit of the devil that

19

the chief priests mocked and invited Jesus to come down from the cross.

If Jesus had come down from the cross, the devil would have won a tremendous victory that day, because the lifting up of Jesus on the cross was an eternal "must" (John 3:14, 15).

They continued by saying, "He trusted in God; let Him deliver Him now if He will have Him, for He said, I am the Son of God" (Matt. 27:43). God could not deliver Jesus from the cross, because God *delivered Him* into the hands of His enemies *to be nailed to the cross.* If God had taken Jesus from the cross, He would have defeated His own plan of salvation. In the Old Testament these scribes and elders had read such words as "the Lamb, led to the slaughter . . . dumb before the shearers . . . wounded for our transgressions . . . bruised for our iniquities." They had read that He would die with the wicked and make His grave with the rich. Many Scriptures in the Old Testament clearly describe the Lord Jesus—what He would do, His ministry—even His birth and all the details of His coming into the world. There was no excuse for these chief priests, scribes, and elders to become tools of the devil, to try to frustrate the plan of God for the redemption of lost souls.

Many times in the inquiry room, while dealing with people who come forward for salvation, we try to help them by reading verses of Scripture, only to have them look at us and say, "I have known that all of my life." Or they will say, "I memorized that when I was a child," or "I have read the Bible and I know much about the Word of God." When people make statements like that, we always tell them that the things they *know* about the Word of God but have not received by faith, will certainly not help them when they stand in the judgment hour. Rather, it will condemn them and bring upon them more severe judgment. Better were it never to have known the way of life than to know that God loved the world and gave Jesus to die for sinners, and then refuse to believe on Him unto salvation.

The Word of God is the power of God unto salvation (Rom. 1:16). Jesus promised freedom from condemnation to all who hear His Word and believe on Him. All who *believe* are free from condemnation and have passed from death unto life; but to hear the Word of God and *reject* it is to be *judged* by the Word: "He that rejecteth me, and receiveth not my words, hath one that judgeth him: *the Word that I have spoken,* the same shall judge him in the last day" (John 12:48). The words of the unholy preachers who said, "He saved others, Himself He cannot save," will stand in the great day of judgment against the men who spoke them.

The Voice of Unholy Repetition

The *third voice* is that of the thieves—*the voice*

of unholy repetition. When the chief priests shouted, "He saved others, Himself He cannot save. If He be the King of Israel let Him come down from the cross and we will believe in Him; He trusted in God, let God deliver Him now if He will have Him, for He said, I am the Son of God," the dying thieves *repeated their words:* ". . . the thieves also which were crucified with Him, *cast the same in His teeth."* Poor fellows! All they could do was to repeat what they had heard. Remember, these men were hanging on two crosses, one on either side of Jesus. They were listening to the religious leaders of the day. We wonder if they thought that perhaps Almighty God would have a little more mercy on them if they united with those religious leaders?

Man is incurably religious. Wherever you find man, he worships something; he has some brand of religion. Perhaps these poor, dying thieves thought they were performing a religious act when they agreed with the chief priests and in essence said, *"Amen* to what you have just said; we agree. If He is what He claims to be, let Him come down from the cross, and we too will believe in Him." They repeated what they heard, what others said, not knowing in their hearts whether it was truth or error.

The damning sin of America is *religion minus Jesus.* Religion is growing in America like wildfire. People by the tens of thousands are joining churches.　One of the most approved things any person can do today is to join a church, especially one of high social standing.　It is very popular to become a church member.　People are invited to "join the church of your choice."　A spiritually minded preacher will never make such an announcement from his pulpit.　God's ministers should invite Christians to join churches where the Word of God is preached in its purity.　We should do our best to lead people into churches that present the shed blood as the only covering for sin.

Dear reader, are you, like so many people, guilty of learning about God and the Bible only from *what someone else* has said?　In other words, do you go to church, do you listen to the preacher; do you go to Sunday school, do you listen to the teacher, but never open the Word of God and search its pages for yourself?　Here is good sound advice:　Get a good Bible, read it, study it, ask God to give you light, and *believe it!*　Do not depend upon someone else to put words into your mouth concerning your belief and your religion.

These poor thieves were not Sunday school boys. They were convicted, condemned criminals who admitted, "We receive our just reward."　They repeated what the religious leaders said about the Man on the middle cross.　Do not be an unholy repeater.　Do not repeat what others have said, unless you know for certain that you are repeating pure truth.

The Voice of Misinterpretation

The record of the *fourth voice* around Calvary is found in Matthew 27:45—47: "Now from the sixth hour there was darkness over all the land unto the ninth hour. And about the ninth hour Jesus cried with a loud voice, saying, Eli, Eli, lama sabachthani? that is to say, My God, my God, why hast thou forsaken me? *Some of them that stood there, when they heard that, said, This Man calleth for Elias.*"

When Jesus cried out, "My God, my God, why hast thou forsaken me?" some of those who stood around the cross said, "This Man calleth for Elias." They misinterpreted the words of Jesus. He was not calling for God to come to the rescue. He was not asking God to take Him from the cross. Hours before, in the Garden of Gethsemane, He had surrendered His will entirely to the Father. His cry from the cross was misinterpreted.

If you are a fundamental Christian, if you believe in the verbal inspiration of the Bible, then you believe in the omnipotence, the omniscience and the omnipresence of God. You also believe that the members of the Godhead are equal. You believe that Jesus was omnipotent, omniscient, and omnipresent. It is true that He was man, but He was *God-man;* therefore Jesus knew every detail of the happenings of Calvary. He did not cry out in surprise when He cried, "My God, my God, why hast thou forsaken me?" He was announcing to

24

the world that God had turned His head while His Son was bearing the sins of the whole wide world in His body. Jesus was not screaming for help. He was making an announcement, the announcement that God had forsaken Him. God cannot look upon sin. God cannot acquit the wicked; He *must* judge sin. Therefore, in order that God might be "just and the Justifier of the ungodly," He had permitted Jesus, who knew no sin, to *become* sin. God made Christ to become sin for us, that we in Christ might be made the righteousness of God (II Cor. 5:21). These poor, religious leaders and people around the cross misinterpreted the cry of the Son of God.

It was *prophesied* that Jesus would be forsaken by God and man. It was prophesied that Jesus would be smitten by God; and had God Almighty not forsaken Jesus while He paid the sin-debt, Jesus would never have died. He would have hung on the cross on and on and on. God, of necessity, forsook Him in order that Jesus might pay sin's debt, and sin's debt is *death!* Jesus died for sinners.

These poor people were not the last ones to misinterpret the Word of God. Over and over again we receive letters that read something like this: "You preach salvation by grace through faith plus nothing. Someone else preaches salvation by grace plus this, minus that, through the other, and on and on. One man on the radio says it is this way; another says it is 'my way!' One church preaches this way, another church preaches the other way. Whom am I to believe?" We always answer those letters by referring them to Romans 3:4: "Let God be true, but every man a liar."

Perhaps you are saying, "But how can we know we are right?" The Bible has the answer: If you are a true believer, if you have fully trusted the Lord Jesus from the heart, this applies to you: "Wherefore also it is contained in the Scripture, Behold, I lay in Sion a chief corner stone, elect, precious; and *he that believeth on Him shall not be confounded*" (I Pet. 2:6).

According to the Word of God, truly born again believers are not confused. If you do not know the Gospel when you hear it, you should certainly examine yourself to see if you have ever been saved. God will not allow a sincere seeker of truth to go untaught. God knows the heart; and when any person seeks Him with the whole heart, He will reveal the truth to that person. "The entrance of (God's) words giveth light" (Psalm 119:130). "If we walk in the light, as He is in the light, we have fellowship one with another, and the blood of Jesus Christ (God's) Son cleanseth us from all sin" (I John 1:7).

Dear friend, if you are honestly seeking the truth, "Ye shall know the truth, and the truth shall make you free"—free from worry, doubt, anxiety and fear. If you live in fear, you have not been made perfect in love. God is love. Christ is God. So if you possess Jesus, you possess perfect love. "There is no fear in love; but perfect love casteth out fear because fear hath torment. He that feareth is not made perfect in love" (I John 4:18).

Bow your head, close your eyes, search your heart, and ask God if you have misinterpreted His plan of redemption.

The Voice of Unholy Curiosity Seekers

The record of the *fifth voice* is found in Matthew 27:48, 49: "And straightway one of them ran, and took a sponge, and filled it with vinegar, and put it on a reed, and gave Him to drink. *The rest said, Let be, let us see whether Elias will come to save Him.*"

Just after Jesus cried, "My God, my God, why hast thou forsaken me," and some of the people around the cross said, "He is calling for Elias," one person—why, we do not know—ran and took a sponge, filled it with vinegar, put it on a reed, and held it up for Jesus to drink. As he was doing this, some of the people said, "Let be, let us see whether Elias will come to save Him." This is *the voice of unholy curiosity seekers.*

Those men are dead, and their dust remains in the grave; but their kind are still with us in great numbers—religious curiosity seekers. Let us illustrate: You find a little church built by the highway of life; there God's humble preacher declares the whole counsel of God—the verbal inspiration of the Scriptures, the virgin birth, the vicarious sufferings of Jesus, atonement through the blood, the second coming of Christ, the Spirit-filled life. You find a little church like that, with a minister like that, and it will not be overcrowded; it is just an ordinary church. But let some religious racketeer announce that he will perform some spectacular act, such as some of the modern wonder-working men announce today; and if something spectacular is promised, there is not a building in the city that will seat the people! We believe in miracles; we certainly do. We have witnessed many since we were saved. We believe in divine healing. If there is any healing at all, it is divine. But we believe in divine healing as set forth in the Bible. We do not believe in making merchandise of sick people; neither do we believe in using the church for a religious show. All this we have said in order to say this:

Let some minister announce that he will put an arm on a man, or raise a dead person out of a casket, or open the eyes of a blind person, and you cannot find a building to seat the people. Folks who are not spiritually minded are filled with curiosity; they want to see something. They will drive a thousand miles to "see something" when they would not walk a city block to hear a good Gospel sermon. That is the reason race tracks draw hundreds of thousands of people who expect some automobile to plunge into the guard rail; they expect to see somebody get killed. They go to see the spectacular. These fellows around the cross cried out, "Let Him alone! Don't bother Him . . . let us see if God really will take Him off of the cross! If that should happen, it would really be something worth seeing; so let Him alone and let's keep close watch on Him and see if God will take Him down!"

Dear friend, experience gleaned from many years of evangelistic preaching across America and in many foreign countries, and dealing with many people in the inquiry room convinces me that one thing which hinders many people from being truly born again is that they come looking for something spectacular. *Salvation* is the *greatest miracle* this side of heaven. Salvation comes only through childlike faith in the finished work of Jesus! Many people come into the inquiry room expecting great "feeling," a thrill or a chill, an icicle up their backbone—but we are not saved by "feelings." We are not saved by some emotional stir; we are not saved by seeing a light, or by witnessing some visible miracle from heaven. "Except ye be *converted* and become as a little child, you shall in no wise enter into the kingdom of God." *Salvation is by faith in the finished work of Jesus Christ.* Souls are plunging into hell, stumbling over the simplicity of redemption while looking for the spectacular promised by some religionists.

Religions of works are growing rapidly. Tell people to *give* something, *be* something, or *do* something to win God's favor, and they accept that. But tell people to believe on the Lord Jesus Christ, without seeing, feeling, or without the spectacular, and that is too hard! They are not willing to accept God's wonderful salvation on such simple terms; but dear friend, if you ever step inside the pearly gates and hear the Father say "Well done," it will be because you, in child-like faith, received the Lord Jesus Christ as your personal Saviour.

Yes, they stood around the cross, and they watched Him, wondering if they would really see something spectacular. Would God *really* take Him off the cross?

One word further before we leave the voice of curiosity: Dear reader, why do you go to church? Do you go because you feel it is a religious duty, a national duty, because you feel that everybody should go to church? Do you go to church for curiosity, simply to see what goes on? Do you go to church to see what the other ladies will be wearing, what the other men will be wearing? If you go to the house of God because of your curiosity, then, my friend, you are heaping damnation upon your poor soul. But if you go to church because you love Jesus, because you believe we are not to forsake the assembling of ourselves together

(Heb. 10:25), then you will be rewarded for your faithful church attendance. We *should* go to church—it is right to go to church; but it is not right to go to church with the wrong motive. If you go to church filled with curiosity, then it would be better if you stayed at home. These men who gazed upon Jesus, wondering what God would do about it, would have been better off had they never been born. They were so close to the Christ, so near His shed blood—and yet their curiosity blinded their eyes to the fact that the Lamb of God was dying on the middle cross—the Lamb of God who came to take away the sin of the world (John 1:29).

The Voice of Sincere Supplication

We turn to another Gospel for the *sixth voice* we hear around the cross of Jesus:

"And one of the malefactors which were hanged railed on Him, saying, If thou be Christ, save thyself and us. But the other answering rebuked him, saying, Dost not thou fear God, seeing thou art in the same condemnation? And we indeed justly; for we receive the due reward of our deeds; but this Man hath done nothing amiss. And he said unto Jesus, *Lord, remember me when thou comest into thy kingdom.* And Jesus said unto him, Verily I say unto thee, To day shalt thou be with me in paradise" (Luke 23:39—43). This sixth voice is *the voice of sincere supplication unto the Lord.*

At the outset, both of the thieves "railed on Jesus." They united in the voice of unholy repetition; they both repeated what the chief priests and elders had said. Could it be that the power of the Gospel softened the heart of one of these criminals as he repeated the Word of God? This Word is quick and powerful and sharper than any two-edged sword. The Word is the power of God unto salvation. It may be that one of these thieves really *heard* what he quoted: "He saved others; Himself He cannot save"—or perhaps it was the seven sayings of Jesus on the cross that changed his mind. Whatever it was, this man uttered the cry of sincere supplication unto the Lord. He was *against* the Man on the middle cross to begin with, but he changed his mind and testified in defense of the Lord Jesus. He rebuked the other thief and said, "Dost thou not fear God?" Perhaps the thief changed his mind when Jesus cried, "My God, my God, why hast thou forsaken me?" Regardless of when he changed his mind, he is now asking his fellow-thief, "Do you not fear God? Do you not see we are in the same condemnation as this Man? And we are dying justly, we are receiving the just reward for our deeds. We had a fair trial, we were convicted, we are condemned. We are dying justly. But this Man has done nothing wrong!"

Did you hear that: *"This Man hath done nothing amiss!"* The thief confessed that Jesus was sinless; that He was perfect! Nothing amiss—not one iota of wrong could be found in Jesus. The thief discovered that Jesus was the sinless Son of God! Upon that discovery he looked at Jesus and said, "Lord, remember me when thou comest into thy kingdom." He prayed *nine words* from a heart of sincere supplication. God answered his prayer and saved him. Jesus said, in answer to his prayer, "Today shalt thou be with me in Paradise! In just a few minutes now I will be going to Paradise; you will go with me. You have made unto me a sincere supplication; I heard your call, and I promised 'Come unto me and I will give you rest, come unto me and I will in no wise cast you out.' I will not cast you out; I will remember you today, when we go to Paradise."

There are those who argue that the thief was not saved and that he did not go to Paradise. But, beloved, we are not to argue the Scriptures. "Let God be true, but every man a liar." Jesus said to the thief, "Today you and I shall go to Paradise." I expect to meet the thief when I arrive in Paradise. I am just as sure he is there as I am sure I am going there.

Dear friend, if you do not belong to the group this voice represents, join it today. If you have never sincerely sought God's mercy, bow your head this moment and call upon the Lord. Ask Him to remember you, ask Him to forgive you and come into your heart. He promised, and He cannot fail. He will answer your sincere supplication. Thank

God for the thief who, in his dying hour, found grace!

Do not do as the thief did, friend, by putting off salvation until you are at the point of death. It could be you will be so busy dying, it could be you will be in so much agony, that you will not be capable of praying. In the many years of our ministry we have met a few folks who died without God, and we tried our best to win them on their death-bed; but they just could not seem to understand. They just could not pray, and they went out into eternity unprepared.

I shall never forget standing by the bed of a dear old gentleman who had never made a profession, who had never united with any church. He was dying. I asked him, "Friend, do you believe Jesus died to save you?" And he answered, "Yes, I do." Then I said to this dying man, "Call on God, ask Him to save you." After a moment of hesitation, with the death-rattle in his throat, he looked up into my face and said, "Preacher, I am too sick to pray!" He died, too sick to pray, and I am sure he plunged to the blackness of darkness forever—into hellfire.

Do not put it off too long. Do not wait until you are too busy dying to pray. Call on God now; He will save you.

The Voice of Heartfelt Confession

And now we come to the *seventh voice* around

34

the cross of Calvary. We turn to another Gospel to study the seventh voice. Beginning with Mark 15:24 we have the outline of the events:

Jesus was on the cross; they had divided His garments and gambled for His coat. They crucified two thieves, one on either side of Him. They that passed by wagged their heads, made faces at Jesus, and cried out, "Save thyself! Come down from the cross!" The chief priests mocked, laughed and sneered; the scribes did the same. About the sixth hour there was total darkness over all the land until the ninth hour. The ninth hour Jesus cried out, "My God, my God, why hast thou forsaken me?" One ran and filled a sponge with vinegar, placed it on a reed, and put it to His lips. Then Jesus cried with a loud voice and gave up the ghost. When He did this, the temple veil was rent in twain from top to bottom, and at that moment the seventh voice sounded:

"And when the centurion, which stood over against Him, saw that He so cried out, and gave up the ghost, he said, *Truly this Man was the Son of God!*" (Mark 15:39).

This seventh voice is *the voice of heartfelt confession.*

The Word of God tells us that the centurion "stood over against Him." Most pictures we see of Calvary place the feet of Jesus several feet off of the ground. Of course, that is only man's idea. Likely the feet of Jesus were very close to the ground, no more than three or four feet from the ground at the most. Therefore, the centurion could literally have stood over against His feet. At any rate, he stood very near.

The centurion had heard so much about this Man. His fame had gone throughout the land because of His mighty works. The centurion wanted to know the truth: he was a sincere seeker of truth. He wanted to know for himself if this Man really was Jesus. He was determined to know, he intended to find out for himself, therefore he took his stand at the foot of the cross and stayed there through it all. He witnessed the mocking, sneering, and jeering of those who passed by. He listened to the cries of mockery and sarcasm, and at the same time he looked into the face of the Lord Jesus and saw the expression on that tender face—not a look of anger or disgust, but a look of intense pity and compassion. He took note of the attitude of Jesus, the look on His face, the forgiving spirit. He was aware of the darkness over all the earth. News spread of the temple veil, rent from top to bottom. Then Jesus cried out and gave up the ghost. That convinced the centurion. He had witnessed the death of enough men to know that a dying man who had been losing blood for hours did not cry out with a loud voice. When Jesus cried with a thunderous voice and then literally gave up the ghost, passing His life back to God, the centurion was thoroughly convinced that he had witnessed the death of the Son of God. He confessed: "Truly, this Man was the Son of God!"

In writing to the Corinthians, Paul clearly states: "Wherefore I give you to understand that no man speaking by the Spirit of God calleth Jesus accursed: and that no man can say that Jesus is the Lord, but by the Holy Ghost" (I Cor. 12:3). The centurion confessed that he had witnessed the death of the Son of God, the Lord Christ. He was convinced in his own heart because he heard the words of Jesus. Romans 10:17 tells us that faith cometh by hearing, and hearing by the Word of God. Jesus tells us if we hear the Word and believe, we are saved. Paul tells us the Word is the power of God unto salvation. The centurion took his position at the feet of Jesus, and he stayed there until he knew the truth. When he knew the truth, he accepted it and was set free. "Ye shall know the truth, and the truth shall make you free" (John 8:32).

I was born again three months before I really knew *how* I was born again. I trusted in all the light I had. I heard God's servant deliver God's Word, and I believed and was saved—but I did not know how. One day I discovered this marvelous verse, and it has been my favorite ever since: "That if thou shalt confess with thy mouth the Lord Jesus, and shalt believe in thine heart that God hath raised Him from the dead, *thou shalt be saved"* (Rom. 10:9). The centurion confessed, "Truly this Man was the Son of God," and undoubtedly he later accepted the fact of the resurrection. The centurion met the conditions of salvation: "Confess with thy mouth the Lord Jesus, believe in thine heart that God raised Him up from the dead—and thou shalt be saved." We have reason to believe that the centurion is resting in Paradise today. Will you sincerely seek the truth, the truth that will set you free and make you a child of God?

In closing, let us become more personal. Will you, dear reader, please identify yourself with the group represented by the voice you display in your daily living? Do you belong to the first group—*the unholy skeptics,* who always say, "If . . ."? What about the second group, *the unholy preachers,* who know so much about the Word of God, who can quote so much Scripture, but who never accept the truth or the Christ of the Scripture? Do you belong to the third group, *the unholy repeaters,* who know only what somebody else has said? Do you repeat what others say, even it if is not true?

The fourth group comprises those who *misinterpret* the Word of God. Instead of reading the Word, letting it say what it says and mean what it means, they put their own interpretation upon it. These people around the cross heard Jesus cry out, "My God, my God, why hast thou for-

38

saken me?" They immediately supposed that He was calling for God to save Him. Instead, He was announcing to the world that God had made Him to become sin so that we poor sinners might become righteous through His death on the cursed tree.

If you have not already done so, please join the sixth group, represented by the thief on the cross who recognized his condition and his need. He also recognized the sinlessness of the Man on the middle cross. He not only recognized the sinlessness of Jesus, but he confessed, "This Man hath done nothing amiss. He should not be dying on a cross." And then he asked the Lord Jesus to remember him, and Jesus did. If you have not asked to be remembered, ask Jesus now. Join the group represented by the sixth voice, and you will automatically confess the words of the seventh voice, the voice of the centurion who so willingly confessed, "This day I have witnessed the death of God's Christ, the Son of God!"

Have you confessed with your mouth that Jesus came into the world, died at the hands of wicked sinners, was buried and rose again the third day according to the Scriptures? (I Cor. 15:1—4). If you have not confessed with your mouth and believed in your heart, *do it now!* He will save you.

To which group do you belong? Dear reader, identify yourself!

SEVEN WORDS

Seven Words

"In the end of the Sabbath, as it began to dawn toward the first day of the week, came Mary Magdalene and the other Mary to see the sepulchre. And, behold, there was a great earthquake: for the angel of the Lord descended from heaven, and came and rolled back the stone from the door, and sat upon it. His countenance was like lightning, and his raiment white as snow: and for fear of him the keepers did shake, and became as dead men. And the angel answered and said unto the women, Fear not ye: for I know that ye seek Jesus, which was crucified. *He is not here: for He is risen,* as He said. Come, see the place where the Lord lay" (Matt. 28:1—6).

"He saith unto them, Be not affrighted: Ye seek Jesus of Nazareth, which was crucified: *He is risen; He is not here:* behold the place where they laid Him" (Mark 16:6).

Seven words—*"He is not here... He is risen!"* Or *"He is risen, He is not here."* These seven words declare the most important truth in all of the Word of God. You may ask, "Could any truth be more important than the truth of the virgin birth? or the cross of Calvary? or the miracles

43

Jesus wrought—healing the sick, giving sight to the blind, and restoring the dead to life? YES! It matters not what Jesus did or who He was, *if hell could have kept Him in the grave, ALL ELSE would have been in vain!*

The Cross and the Resurrection

The cross and the resurrection of the Lord Jesus are inseparable—one demands the other. If Jesus had not died there would of course be no resurrection, hence no faith, no salvation, no new creation; but had he not *conquered* death, hell, and the grave His death would have been in vain. Therefore those who deny His resurrection might just as well deny that He was crucified!

The devil did everything in his ungodly power to keep Jesus from the cross. He knew that if the Son of God reached Calvary, His death on the cross would eventually lead to the bruising of the serpent's head (Gen. 3:15) and bring about the downfall of his kingdom.

Hear these words from Ezekiel 28:12—15: ". . . Thou sealest up the sum, full of wisdom, and perfect in beauty. Thou hast been in Eden the garden of God; every precious stone was thy covering, the sardius, topaz, and the diamond, the beryl, the onyx, and the jasper, the sapphire, the emerald, and the carbuncle, and gold: the workmanship of thy tabrets and of thy pipes was prepared in thee in the day that thou wast created. Thou art the

44

anointed cherub that covereth; and I have set thee so: thou wast upon the holy mountain of God; thou hast walked up and down in the midst of the stones of fire. Thou wast perfect in thy ways from the day that thou wast created, till iniquity was found in thee."

The personality described in these verses is the personality known today as the devil, *Satan.* Next to the Godhead he was probably the most powerful person in the universe *until iniquity was found in him.* Isaiah 14:12—15 describes the character of this creature and tells of the "iniquity" mentioned by Ezekiel:

"How art thou fallen from heaven, O Lucifer, son of the morning! How art thou cut down to the ground, which didst weaken the nations! For thou hast said in thine heart, I WILL ascend into heaven, I WILL exalt my throne above the stars of God: I WILL sit also upon the mount of the congregation, in the sides of the north: I WILL ascend above the heights of the clouds; *I WILL be like the Most High!* Yet thou shalt be brought down to hell, to the sides of the pit."

Satan marshalled all the forces of the underworld in an all-out attempt to destroy the Seed of the woman before He reached the cross, but the Son of God, "having spoiled principalities and powers...made a shew of them openly, triumphing over them in it" (Col. 2:15). When Jesus prayed in the Garden of Gethsemane, He saw all the forces of

45

the underworld allied together to crush Him; but God sent an angel to strengthen Him and He won the victory, putting hell to an open shame. (Please study Psalm 22 and Matthew 26:36—46.)

The devil tried to kill Jesus on the Roman whipping post—and failed. He tried to kill Him under the weight of the cross—and failed. The Son of God came into the world to die on the cross, and all the forces of hell could not stop Him! Even after He reached the cross and died there, poor ignorant men thought they could keep Him in the tomb by rolling a heavy stone across the door, sealing it with the imperial seal of Rome, and placing a Roman guard over it (Matt. 27:62—66). But they did not reckon on the power of God and the fact that it was not possible for death to hold Him who was God in flesh. (Read John 1:3, 4 and Acts 2:24.)

It *was not possible* that death should hold the Son of God! Death is the result of sin—"The wages of sin is death" (Rom. 6:23), "Sin, when it is finished, bringeth forth death" (James 1:15)—but Jesus did not sin, there was no sin in Him. *Therefore death had NO CLAIM on Him!* Jesus did not die as mortals die; He did not die a "natural" death. *He laid His life down of Himself,* that He might take it again. In His discourse on the Good Shepherd He testified, *"Therefore doth my Father love me, because I lay down my life, that I might take it again. NO MAN TAKETH IT FROM ME, but I LAY IT DOWN OF MYSELF. I have power*

46

to lay it down, and I have power to take it again. This commandment have I received of my Father" (John 10:17, 18).

Jesus is LIFE, and it is impossible for death to hold life. He took a body in order that He might die, lay His life down, and *through death* make eternal life possible for all who believe. "We see Jesus, who was made a little lower than the angels for the suffering of death, crowned with glory and honour; that He *by the grace of God* should taste death *for every man"* (Heb. 2:9).

Death is not the cessation of existence, it is not the extension of being. Death is the *tearing asunder* of soul and spirit from the body. In Psalm 16:10 we read, "Thou wilt not leave *my soul* in hell; neither wilt thou suffer thine Holy One to see *corruption."* When Jesus died on the cross He said to the Father, "Into thy hands I commend my spirit" (Luke 23:46). In other words, Jesus literally took His life in His own hands and passed it into the hands of God in heaven. *No man killed Jesus!* It is true that men demanded His death, men arrested and condemned Him, and the hands of wicked men nailed Him to the cross—but make no mistake, beloved, *man DID NOT take His life!* Had Jesus not given His life back into the Father's hands, He would still be hanging on the cross to-day—*alive.* He was God in flesh, and *GOD cannot die.*

Jesus gave His *spirit* to the heavenly Father,

Pilate gave the Lord's lifeless body to Nicodemus and Joseph of Arimathaea. They took it down from the cross and placed it in Joseph's new tomb—but it was not possible for corruption to destroy His body, and on the third day after His burial Jesus came forth from the grave *in the same body* Nicodemus and Joseph had placed in the tomb! If He *had not* risen bodily He would not have won total victory over death. He *could* have gone back to heaven *without* a body, He was with the Father "in the beginning" without a body—He was the Word, in the bosom of the Father (John 1:1, 14, 18). He received His body from the Virgin Mary, but His blood was the blood of God the eternal Father (Luke 1:34, 35; Acts 20:28).

The *Christ of God* was not *born*—He was in the beginning with God; but *Jesus the Man* was born about two thousand years ago, in a body of humiliation in which He was to die and thus pay the sin-debt for all mankind, for whosoever would accept His finished work in faith believing. Therefore without His *bodily resurrection* He would have won only partial victory over death. But *He did rise bodily,* and God's Word declares:

"When this corruptible shall have put on incorruption, and this mortal shall have put on immortality, then shall be brought to pass the saying that is written, *Death is swallowed up in victory.* O death, where is thy sting? O grave, where is thy victory? The sting of death is sin; and the strength

48

of sin is the law. *But thanks be to God, which giveth us the victory THROUGH OUR LORD JESUS CHRIST!"* (I Cor. 15:54—57).

Thank God, Jesus did not stop short of total victory—victory over the world, the flesh, and the devil, death, hell, and the grave. He took a body that was capable of dying, and in that body He died and rose again. His bodily resurrection is the guarantee that He conquered all He came to conquer, and He now holds "the keys of hell and of death" (Rev. 1:18).

Christ's Bodily Resurrection
Is the Grounds For Saving Faith

"Now if Christ be preached that He rose from the dead, how say some among you that there is no resurrection of the dead? But if there be no resurrection of the dead, then is Christ not risen: and if Christ be not risen, then is our preaching vain, and your faith is also vain. Yea, and we are found false witnesses of God; because we have testified of God that He raised up Christ: whom He raised not up, if so be that the dead rise not. For if the dead rise not, then is not Christ raised: and if Christ be not raised, your faith is vain; ye are yet in your sins. Then they also which are fallen asleep in Christ are perished. If in this life only we have hope in Christ we are of all men most miserable.

"But now is Christ risen from the dead, and

49

become the firstfruits of them that slept. For since by man came death, by man came also the resurrection of the dead. For as in Adam all die, even so in Christ shall all be made alive. But every man in his own order: Christ the firstfruits; afterward they that are Christ's at His coming.

"Then cometh the end, when He shall have delivered up the kingdom to God, even the Father; when He shall have put down all rule and all authority and power. For He must reign, till He hath put all enemies under His feet. The last enemy that shall be destroyed is death" (I Cor. 15:12—26).

In the days of Christ's earthly ministry, the group of religionists who did not believe in the resurrection were called Sadducees (Matt. 22:23—33). People who hold to the same false doctrine are with us today, but they are no longer called Sadducees. They have several different denominational names, they have big churches with high steeples, and from all outward appearances they look like real Bible Christians. But anyone who denies the bodily resurrection of Jesus is *not* a Christian. This statement is based on the Word of God, for Paul declares under inspiration, *"If Christ be NOT risen, then is our preaching vain, and your FAITH is also vain!"*

It matters not how fervently men may preach the love of God, the grace of God, the mercy of God. If Christ did not rise from the dead, the message is empty and worthless. The heart, soul, and bloodstream of the Gospel is the resurrection of Jesus *"according to the Scriptures."* To the Corinthian believers Paul defined the Gospel he preached. In I Corinthians 15:1—4 he said:

"Moreover, brethren, I declare unto you *the GOSPEL which I preached unto you,* which also ye have received, and wherein ye stand, by which also ye are saved, if ye keep in memory what I preached unto you, unless ye have believed in vain. For I delivered unto you first of all *that which I also RECEIVED, how that CHRIST DIED FOR OUR SINS according to the Scriptures; and that HE WAS BURIED, and that HE ROSE AGAIN THE THIRD DAY according to the Scriptures."*

Paul preached what he himself had received— i. e., that Christ died, was buried, and rose again the third day—NOT according to the chief priests or the religious leaders, but *according to THE SCRIPTURES!* So—the Gospel which Paul received and which He preached is *the DEATH, BURIAL, and RESURRECTION of Jesus according to the Word of God.*

When did Paul receive this message? The record is given in Acts chapter 9. Paul (at that time *Saul of Tarsus*) was traveling to Damascus to arrest Christians in that city and bring them back to Jerusalem to stand trial for their faith. But just outside the Damascus gate, a bright light from heaven shone round about Paul, "and he fell to the earth, and heard a voice saying unto him, Saul, Saul, why persecutest thou me? And he said, Who art thou, Lord? And the Lord said, I am Jesus whom thou persecutest: it is hard for thee to kick against the pricks.

"And he trembling and astonished said, Lord, what wilt thou have me to do? And the Lord said unto him, Arise, and go into the city, and it shall be told thee what thou must do. And the men which journeyed with him stood speechless, hearing a voice, but seeing no man. And Saul arose from the earth; and when his eyes were opened, he saw no man: but they led him by the hand, and brought him into Damascus. And he was three days without sight, and neither did eat nor drink" (Acts 9:1—9). Saul followed the instructions of Jesus without question—*and all who hope to be saved must do the same.*

Paul's companions led him by the hand and took him the rest of the way into Damascus, to the house of a man named Judas. The Lord then spoke to a disciple named Ananias and told him to go and talk with Paul. Ananias at first hesitated, for he knew the reputation of Saul of Tarsus as persecutor of the Church; but God assured him that no harm would come to him and that Paul was a chosen vessel to bear the Gospel to the Gentiles, and to suffer "great things" for the sake of Christ. Then in verses 17—20 in Acts chapter 9 we read:

"And Ananias went his way, and entered into the house; and putting his hands on him said,

Brother Saul, *the Lord, even JESUS*, that appeared unto thee in the way as thou camest, hath sent me, that thou mightest receive thy sight, and be filled with the Holy Ghost. And immediately there fell from his eyes as it had been scales: and he received sight forthwith, and arose, and was baptized. And when he had received meat he was strengthened. Then was Saul certain days with the disciples which were at Damascus. *And straightway HE PREACHED CHRIST in the synagogues, that He is the Son of God."*

From the time Saul asked, "Lord, what wilt thou have me to do?" he listened and let Jesus do the talking. It is true that Saul's conversion was spectacular, but from the standpoint of true conversion he was saved as all sinners must be saved — simply by hearing and obeying the Word of God. He put his faith in the crucified, buried, risen Lord, and that very moment Saul the persecutor became Paul the apostle — preacher, soul-winner, and, eventually, martyr for the cause of Christ! His message was always the death, burial, and resurrection of Jesus — "according to the Scriptures." Faith comes by hearing, and hearing by the Word of God. *There IS no other way to be saved.* Let the Scripture speak for itself:

"Whosoever shall call upon the name of the Lord shall be saved. How then shall they call on Him in whom they have not believed? and how shall they believe in Him of whom they have not

heard? and how shall they hear without a preacher? and how shall they preach, except they be sent? As it is written, How beautiful are the feet of them that preach the Gospel of peace and bring glad tidings of good things! But they have not all obeyed the Gospel. For Esaias saith, Lord, who hath believed our report? So then, FAITH cometh by HEARING, and HEARING by THE WORD OF GOD" (Rom. 10:13—17).

Notice: The invitation is to *"whosoever" will call* upon the name of the Lord—but no one will call until he *believes*, and no one can *believe* until he first *hears* the Word of God. Thus the Word of God must be *preached* before it can be *heard*, and "how shall they *preach, except they be SENT?"* (*"Sent"* preachers are God-called, God-anointed men who preach the same message Paul preached— the death, burial, and resurrection of the Lord Jesus Christ, "according to the Scriptures.")

So we see God's plan for saving souls. He calls preachers and sends them to preach the Word to lost mankind. Unbelievers hear and believe the Word, faith prompts them to call on Jesus for salvation, and Jesus saves the soul that calls on Him in faith.

The Bodily Resurrection of Jesus— the Seal of Truth

Concerning prophecies of His Incarnation:—
Christ's bodily resurrection is the seal of truth

stamped upon all that the prophets prophesied concerning His coming into the world. All of the Old Testament prophets foretold the suffering of the Messiah and the glory that should follow. Jesus made this very plain when, after His resurrection, He joined the disciples on the way to Emmaus as they were discussing His crucifixion and the disappointment of their high hopes. They said, "We trusted that it had been He which should have redeemed Israel." Jesus said to them, "O fools, and slow of heart to believe *all that the prophets have spoken!* Ought not Christ to have suffered these things, and to enter into His glory? *And beginning at Moses and all the prophets, He expounded unto them in all the Scriptures the things concerning Himself*" (Luke 24:21–27). All of the prophecies concerning Him would have been false if He had not risen from the dead—*bodily.*

Concerning what Jesus said
about His resurrection:—

The bodily resurrection of Jesus is the seal of truth concerning all that He Himself said about His resurrection:

In John 2:19, 21 He said, "Destroy this temple, and *in three days I will raise it up.* (He spake of the temple of His body.)"

In Matthew 16:21 we read, "From that time forth began Jesus to shew unto His disciples how that He must go unto Jerusalem, and suffer many things of the elders and chief priests and scribes, and be killed, *and be raised again the third day.*"

In Matthew 17:22, 23 we read, "While they abode in Galilee, Jesus said unto them, The Son of man shall be betrayed into the hands of men: *and they shall kill Him, and the third day He shall be raised again.* And they (the disciples) were exceeding sorry."

Jesus had called these twelve men to minister with Him, and for more than three years they had walked and talked with Him. They witnessed His mighty miracles, they heard His wonderful words of life, they were present with Him when He healed all manner of diseases and raised the dead. But they did not understand the full meaning of His words when He told them that He would go into Jerusalem, that He would be arrested, tried, condemned, and put to death—but that *He would conquer death and RISE AGAIN the third day.* "They were exceeding sorry," and their sadness was evident to Jesus. He comforted them with these precious words of assurance:

"Let not your heart be troubled: ye believe in God, believe also in me. In my Father's house are many mansions: if it were not so, I would have told you. I go to prepare a place for you. And if I go and prepare a place for you, I will come again, and receive you unto myself; that where I am, there ye may be also. And whither I go ye know, and the way ye know. Thomas saith unto

Him, Lord, we know not whither thou goest; and how can we know the way? Jesus saith unto him, I AM THE WAY, the TRUTH, and the LIFE: No man cometh unto the Father, but by me" (John 14:1—6).

If Jesus had not risen from the dead, all of these promises would have failed, these Scriptures would be false, and He, the living Word, would not have been Truth. The disciples were confused and broken-hearted, discouraged and disappointed. In spite of the words of assurance their Lord had given them, the moment He was arrested most of them fled in mortal fear; and soon thereafter Peter turned back to his fishing nets, taking six of the other disciples with him (John 21:2, 3). Their faith was shaken. They never expected to see their blessed Lord again, and when He appeared to them in the upper room after His resurrection "they were terrified and affrighted, and supposed that they had seen a spirit."

Then Jesus said to them, "Why are ye troubled? and why do thoughts arise in your hearts? Behold my hands and my feet, that it is I myself: handle me, and see; for *a spirit hath not flesh and bones*, as ye see me have.

"And when He had thus spoken, He shewed them His hands and His feet. And while they yet believed not for joy, and wondered, He said unto them, *Have ye here any meat?* And they gave Him a piece of a broiled fish, and of an honeycomb.

And He took it, and did eat before them.

"And He said unto them: *These are the words which I spake unto you, while I was yet with you,* that all things must be fulfilled, which were written in the law of Moses, and in the prophets, and in the psalms, concerning me. Then opened He their understanding, that they might understand the Scriptures" (Luke 24:36—45).

I repeat: If Jesus had not risen *bodily* from the grave, everything He said to His disciples about His resurrection, every promise He made concerning the life to come, would have been false. Therefore His bodily resurrection was God's seal of truth on what He Himself had declared.

Concerning Christ's authority as universal Judge:—

Acts 17:31 tells us that God "hath appointed a day, in the which He will judge the world in righteousness *by that Man whom He hath ordained;* whereof He hath given assurance unto all men, in that He hath *raised Him from the dead.*"

"For the Father judgeth no man, but hath committed all judgment unto the Son" (John 5:22).

Yes, Christ's bodily resurrection was a divine imperative as the seal of truth concerning His authority as universal Judge.

Concerning the bodily resurrection of believers:—

"If the Spirit of Him that raised up Jesus from the dead dwell in you, He that raised up Christ from the dead shall also quicken your mortal bodies by His Spirit that dwelleth in you" (Rom. 8:11).

The bodily resurrection of the Lord Jesus Christ is the seal of truth which guarantees *our* bodily resurrection. In I Thessalonians 4:14 we read, "If we believe that *Jesus died and ROSE AGAIN, even so them also which sleep in Jesus will God bring with Him.*"

Because HE lives, WE live. He conquered death, and believers are *MORE than conquerors* through Him (Rom. 8:37).

*Concerning the Person and
the Word of God's beloved Son:—*

The Apostle Paul opens his letter to the Roman believers with these words:

"Paul, a servant of Jesus Christ, called to be an apostle, separated unto the Gospel of God, which He had promised afore by His prophets in the Holy Scriptures, *concerning His Son Jesus Christ our Lord,* which was made of the seed of David according to the flesh; and *declared to be the Son of God WITH POWER, according to the Spirit of holiness, BY THE RESURRECTION FROM THE DEAD*" (Rom. 1:1—4).

The prophets prophesied concerning the Son of God, that He would be of the seed of David "according to the *flesh,*" He was "declared to be the Son of God *with power,*" and by His bodily resurrection from the dead God put His seal of truth on the Person and the Word of His only begotten

Son. *Jesus IS truth.*

Christ's Resurrection Is the Foundation of New Life For Believers

"Of (God) are ye in Christ Jesus, who of God is made unto us wisdom, and righteousness, and sanctification, and redemption" (I Cor. 1:30).

Salvation is much, much more than redemption from the damnation of hell. It is true that Christ died for our sins (I Cor. 15:3). We are redeemed by His blood (I Pet. 1:18, 19), and delivered from the wrath to come (I Thess. 1:10). But salvation is more than these things. Christ is not only our RE-DEEMER—*He is REDEMPTION!* He not only makes us *right with God*—He is *our RIGHTEOUS-NESS.* "For what saith the Scripture: Abraham *believed God,* and it was counted (imputed) unto him for *righteousness*" (Rom. 4:3).

Righteousness is not attained. It is *imputed.* Believers are righteous only because the righteousness of Christ is imputed to us when we exercise faith in His finished work. Righteousness is not of works, no matter how "righteous" the works may be. Righteousness is not keeping the law or living by the Golden Rule. Righteousness is *CHRIST IN YOU, the hope of glory* (Col. 1:27).

"But now the righteousness of God without the law is manifested, being witnessed by the law and the prophets; *even the righteousness of God which is by faith of Jesus Christ unto all and upon all them that believe:* for there is no difference: For ALL have sinned, and come short of the glory of God; being justified freely by His grace through the redemption that is in Christ Jesus: whom God hath set forth to be a propitiation through faith in His blood, to declare His righteousness for the remission of sins that are past, through the forbearance of God; to declare, I say, at this time His righteousness: that He might be just, and the Justifier of him which believeth in Jesus.

"Where is boasting then? It is excluded. By what law? Of works? Nay: but by the law of faith. *THEREFORE we conclude that a man is justified by faith WITHOUT the deeds of the law"* (Rom. 3:21—28).

Being redeemed by the blood of the Lamb is no ordinary transaction. It is the greatest miracle since the virgin birth of Jesus. Salvation is more than subtraction and addition—i. e., when a person is saved he does not simply *"subtract" the world* and *"add" good living.* He does not just replace wrong with right. To be *saved* is to be *born of God,* born from above (John 1:12,13; 3:3,5). The new birth takes place through the spiritual "seed" —the Word of God (I Pet. 1:23). The new birth is the result of receiving "the engrafted Word" (James 1:21); and the *born one* then becomes a partaker of DIVINE NATURE (II Pet. 1:4). *"THEREFORE if any man be in Christ, he is a NEW CREATURE: old things are passed away; behold, all*

61

things are become new" (II Cor. 5:17).

Saving faith brings us into union with Christ—not on a "business" basis, but on a very *personal* basis:

The believer is "IN Christ Jesus" (Rom. 8:1).

Christ is IN the believer—"Christ in YOU, the hope of glory" (Col. 1:27).

The believer is "hid WITH CHRIST in God" (Col. 3:3).

In Christ, the believer possesses "the righteousness of God" (II Cor. 5:21).

In Christ, the believer is "justified *by the faith of Christ"* (Gal. 2:16).

In Christ, the believer is acceptable to God—*"accepted IN THE BELOVED"* (Eph. 1:6).

The believer is the creation of the mighty hands and miracle-working power of the Lord Jesus Christ: "For BY GRACE are ye saved through faith; and that not of yourselves: it is the gift of God: not of works, lest any man should boast. *For we are HIS workmanship, created IN CHRIST JESUS unto good works,* which God hath before ordained that we should walk in them" (Eph. 2:8—10).

Being a Christian is not simply being "religious." To be a Christian is *to know Christ* and to *possess* Christ. Christianity is knowing *a PERSON,* not a *program.* Paul testified, *"I know WHOM I have believed,* and am persuaded that He is able to keep that which I have committed unto Him against that day" (II Tim. 1:12).

The Bodily Resurrection of Jesus —
the Basis for the Transfiguration of the World

"For I reckon that the sufferings of this present time are not worthy to be compared with the glory which shall be revealed in us. For the earnest expectation of the creature waiteth for the manifestation of the sons of God. For the creature was made subject to vanity, not willingly, but by reason of Him who hath subjected the same in hope. Because the creature itself also shall be delivered from the bondage of corruption into the glorious liberty of the children of God. For we know that the whole creation groaneth and travaileth in pain together until now. And not only they, but ourselves also, which have the firstfruits of the Spirit, even we ourselves groan within ourselves, waiting for the adoption, to wit, the redemption of our body" (Rom. 8:18—23).

God did not create this earth to be under a curse, He did not create it "without form and void." He created this earth for His glory, to be inhabited by man made in God's image. One day the curse will be lifted, there will be peace on earth and good will among men, and this earth will be one great Garden of Eden! This will take place when Jesus sits on the throne of David and reigns in righteousness—and this could never be if He had not risen from the dead.

In Paul's sermon in the synagogue in Antioch in Pisidia, he reminded the Jews of God's promise that through the seed of David He would raise up a Saviour:

"Men of Israel, and ye that fear God, give audience. The God of this people of Israel chose our fathers, and exalted the people when they dwelt as strangers in the land of Egypt, and with an high arm brought He them out of it. And about the time of forty years suffered He their manners in the wilderness. And when He had destroyed seven nations in the land of Chanaan, He divided their land to them by lot. And after that He gave unto them judges about the space of four hundred and fifty years, until Samuel the prophet. And afterward they desired a king: and God gave unto them Saul the son of Cis, a man of the tribe of Benjamin, by the space of forty years.

"And when He had removed him, He raised up unto them David to be their king; to whom also He gave testimony, and said, I have found David the son of Jesse, a man after mine own heart, which shall fulfil all my will. *OF THIS MAN'S SEED hath God according to His promise raised unto Israel a Saviour, Jesus:* when John had first preached before His coming the baptism of repentance to all the people of Israel. And as John fulfilled his course, he said, Whom think ye that I am? I am not He. But, behold, there cometh One after me, whose shoes of His feet I am not worthy to loose.

"Men and brethren, children of the stock of

Abraham, and whosoever among you feareth God, to you is the word of this salvation sent. For they that dwell at Jerusalem, and their rulers, because they knew Him not, nor yet the voices of the prophets which are read every sabbath day, they have fulfilled them in condemning Him. And though they found no cause of death in Him, yet desired they Pilate that He should be slain. And when they had fulfilled all that was written of Him, they took Him down from the tree, and laid Him in a sepulchre.

"BUT GOD RAISED HIM FROM THE DEAD! And He was seen many days of them which came up with Him from Galilee to Jerusalem, who are His witnesses unto the people. And we declare unto you glad tidings, how that THE PROMISE which was made UNTO THE FATHERS, God hath FULFILLED THE SAME unto us their children, in that He hath RAISED UP JESUS AGAIN; as it is also written in the second psalm, Thou art my Son, this day have I begotten thee. And as concerning that He raised Him up from the dead, now no more to return to corruption, He said on this wise, *I will give you the sure mercies of David.* Wherefore He saith also in another psalm, Thou shalt not suffer thine Holy One to see corruption. For David, after he had served his own generation by the will of God, fell on sleep, and was laid unto his fathers, and saw corruption: but *He whom God raised again saw no corruption.*

"Be it known unto you therefore, men and brethren, that through this Man is preached unto you the forgiveness of sins: and by Him all that believe are justified from all things, from which ye could not be justified by the law of Moses" (Acts 13:16—39).

Since Jesus conquered death, hell, and the grave, *His bodily resurrection is the GUARANTEE that every promise made to David will be kept to the letter!* It was not possible that death should hold Him, His body did not see corruption, and His resurrection gives assurance that this earth will one day be delivered from the curse. *The promised kingdom WILL COME!*

By like token, the covenant God made with *Abraham* many centuries ago will be fulfilled exactly as God promised. In Genesis 12:1—3 we read:

"Now the Lord had said unto Abram, Get thee out of thy country, and from thy kindred, and from thy father's house, unto a land that I will shew thee: and I will make of thee a great nation, and I will bless thee, and make thy name great; and thou shalt be a blessing: and I will bless them that bless thee, and curse him that curseth thee: and in thee shall all families of the earth be blessed."

God made a definite promise to Abraham, a promise not yet entirely fulfilled and which could never be fulfilled had not Jesus risen from the grave. Through the promise God made to Abraham, he and his descendants became *the heirs of promise*. God's covenant with Abraham was wholly gracious and unconditional. However, in order to receive the blessing promised, God's chosen people were to remain in their own country. They lost the blessing when they went down into Egypt, but they did not lose their covenant.

The *Dispensation of Promise* ended when Israel accepted the law. The *Dispensation of Law* began when they said, *"All that the Lord hath spoken we will DO"* (Ex. 19:8). The law was given to Israel, and to Israel alone. Therefore it must be distinguished from the covenant God made with Abraham. The *law* was a mode of testing. The *covenant* is unconditional and everlasting.

The law did not abrogate the covenant God made with Abraham. Paul makes this very plain in Galatians 3:16—18: "Now to Abraham and his seed were the promises made. He saith not, And to *seeds*, as of many; but as of *one*, And *to thy SEED*, which is Christ. And this I say, that the covenant, that was confirmed before of God in Christ, *the law* (which was four hundred and thirty years after) *cannot disannul*, that it should make the promise of none effect. For if the inheritance be of the law, it is no more of promise: but God gave it to Abraham by promise."

The law was an intermediate disciplinary dealing with Israel "till the Seed (Jesus) should come to whom the promise was made." This, too, is expressed in Paul's letter to the Galatians:

"Wherefore then serveth the law? *It was added because of transgressions,* till the Seed should come to whom the promise was made; and it was ordained by angels in the hand of a mediator. Now a mediator is not a mediator of one, but God is one.

"Is the law then *against the promises of God?* God forbid! For if there had been a law given which could have given life, verily righteousness should have been by the law. But the Scripture hath concluded all under sin, that the promise by faith of Jesus Christ might be given to them that believe. But *before faith came,* we were kept under the law, shut up unto the faith which should afterwards be revealed. *Wherefore the law was our schoolmaster to bring us unto Christ, that we might be justified by faith.* But after that faith is come, we are no longer under a schoolmaster.

"For ye are all the children of God by faith in Christ Jesus. For as many of you as have been baptized into Christ have put on Christ. There is neither Jew nor Greek, there is neither bond nor free, there is neither male nor female: for ye are all one in Christ Jesus. And *if ye be Christ's, then are ye Abraham's seed, and heirs according to the promise.*

"Now I say, That the heir, as long as he is a child, differeth nothing from a servant, though he be lord of all; but is under tutors and governors until the time appointed of the father. Even so we, when we were children, were in bondage under the elements of the world: but when the fulness of the time was come, God sent forth His Son, made of a woman, made under the law, to redeem them that were under the law, that we might receive the adoption of sons. And because ye are sons, God hath sent forth the Spirit of His Son into your hearts, crying, Abba, Father. Wherefore thou art no more a servant, but a son; and if a son, then an heir of God through Christ" (Gal. 3:19—4:7).

In Genesis 12:1—3 the Abrahamic Covenant is given *as formed*. It is confirmed in Genesis 13:14—17, also in Genesis 15:18, and again in Genesis 17:1—8 where we read: "When Abram was ninety years old and nine, the Lord appeared to Abram, and said unto him: *I am the Almighty God; walk before me, and be thou perfect. And I will make my covenant between me and thee, and will multiply thee exceedingly.*

"And Abram fell on his face; and God talked with him, saying: As for me, behold, my covenant is with thee, and thou shalt be a father of many nations. Neither shall thy name any more be called Abram, but thy name shall be Abraham; for a father of many nations have I made thee. And I will make thee exceeding fruitful, and I will make nations of thee, and kings shall come out of thee. And I will establish my covenant between me and thee and thy seed after thee in their generations for an *everlasting covenant,* to be a God unto thee, and to thy seed after thee. And I will give unto thee, and to thy seed after thee, the land wherein thou art a stranger, all the land of Canaan, for *an everlasting possession;* and I will be their God."

The everlasting covenant God made with Abraham is in seven distinct parts, and without the bodily resurrection of Jesus (the promised Seed) the covenant could not have been fulfilled in its entirety.

Let us notice briefly the seven parts of the Abrahamic Covenant:

1. *"I will make of thee a great nation."* This was to be fulfilled in a natural posterity "as the dust of the earth" (Gen. 13:16). Israel did multiply, even in the face of persistent attempts by other nations to destroy the nation. When God gives Israel the promised kingdom, their children will be "as the stars of the heaven, and as the sand which is upon the sea shore" (Gen. 22:17).

2. *"I will bless thee."* God has kept this promise, in temporal as well as spiritual things; and He will keep it to an even greater degree in the future kingdom. For the temporal blessings God showered on Abraham and his descendants, read Genesis 13:14–17, 15:18, and 24:34, 35.

But God gave spiritual blessings as well. In Genesis 15:6 we are told that Abraham "believed in the Lord; and He counted it to him for righteousness." Paul repeats this in Romans 4:3. Then in John 8:56 Jesus said to the *unbelieving* Jews, "Your father Abraham rejoiced to see my day: and he saw it, and was glad."

In Paul's letter to the Romans he speaks of them "who also walk in the steps of that faith of our father Abraham, which he had being yet uncircumcised. For the *promise*, that he should be the heir of the world, was not to Abraham or to his seed through the *law*, but *through THE RIGHTEOUSNESS OF FAITH*. For if they which are of the law be heirs, faith is made void, and the promise made of none effect.... Therefore it is of faith, that it might be by grace; to the end the promise might be sure to all the seed; not to that only which is of the law, but to that also which is of the faith of Abraham; who is the father of us all. . . . He staggered not at the promise of God through unbelief; but was *strong in faith*, giving glory to God; and being fully persuaded that, *what He had promised, HE WAS ABLE ALSO TO PERFORM*. And therefore it was imputed to him for righteousness" (Rom. 4:12−22 in part).

3. *"I will...make thy name great."* Abraham's name *is* great. It is a *universal* name among Christians, and Abraham is the only Old Testament character mentioned in the New Testament illustration of the peace and rest of Paradise! The beggar Lazarus of Luke 16 was carried by the angels "into Abraham's bosom"−which is the symbol of the place of rest.

4. *"Thou shalt be a blessing."* This promise, too, has been kept, for it was through the seed of

Abraham that our precious Saviour came: "Christ hath redeemed us from the curse of the law, being made a curse for us: for it is written, Cursed is every one that hangeth on a tree: *that the BLESS-ING OF ABRAHAM might come on the Gentiles through Jesus Christ; that we might receive the promise of the Spirit through faith"* (Gal. 3:13, 14). Through Christ (the promised Seed) Abraham is *still* blessing all who will have faith in Christ's finished work; but if Christ had not risen from the dead we would have no faith and there would be no salvation.

5. *"I will bless them that bless thee."* All anyone need do to see whether or not this is true is to study the history of the Jewish nation. Every nation or country that has been friendly toward the Jew has been blessed abundantly, and every nation that has attempted to *stamp out* the Jew has suffered defeat! The same is true in this very hour. There is no doubt that one of the reasons America is the greatest nation on earth today is that she has been—and still is—a friend to the nation of Israel. God has never broken a promise, and He never will.

6. *"I will...curse him that curseth thee."* Down through the centuries since the Jewish nation came into being, other nations have attempted to destroy Israel. But in every instance, those who have tried to wipe out the Jews have gone down in defeat! Hitler declared that he would not be happy until every Jew was destroyed. Hitler is dead, his great

war machine is crushed, while the Jews continue to multiply by the millions! The day will come when all men will follow the Jew to the Holy City, and Jerusalem will be the center of worship for the entire world:

"Thus saith the Lord of hosts: It shall yet come to pass, that there shall come people, and the inhabitants of many cities: and the inhabitants of one city shall go to another, saying, Let us go speedily to pray before the Lord, and to seek the Lord of hosts: I will go also. Yea, many people and strong nations shall come to seek the Lord of hosts *in Jerusalem,* and to pray before the Lord.

"Thus saith the Lord of hosts: In those days it shall come to pass, that ten men shall take hold out of all languages of the nations, even shall take hold of the skirt of him that is a Jew, saying, We will go with you: for we have heard that God is with you" (Zech. 8:20−23).

The future will prove this principle even more remarkably. In Deuteronomy 30:7 we read, "The Lord thy God will put all these curses upon thine enemies, and on them that hate thee, which persecuted thee."

Isaiah 14:1 prophesies, "The Lord will have mercy on Jacob, and will yet choose Israel, and set them in their own land: and the strangers shall be joined with them, and they shall cleave to the house of Jacob."

Hear the prophecy of Joel concerning the restoration of Israel and God's judgment upon their enemies:

"For, behold, in those days, and in that time, when I shall bring again the captivity of Judah and Jerusalem, I will also gather all nations, and will bring them down into the valley of Jehoshaphat, and will plead with them there for my people and for my heritage Israel, whom they have scattered among the nations, and parted my land. And they have cast lots for my people; and have given a boy for an harlot, and sold a girl for wine, that they might drink. . . .

"Because ye have taken my silver and my gold, and have carried into your temples my goodly pleasant things: the children also of Judah and the children of Jerusalem have ye sold unto the Grecians, that ye might remove them far from their border. Behold, I will raise them out of the place whither ye have sold them, and will return your recompence upon your own head: and I will sell your sons and your daughters into the hand of the children of Judah, and they shall sell them to the Sabeans, to a people far off: for the Lord hath spoken it" (Joel 3:1—8 in part).

In Micah 5:7—9 God promises, "The remnant of Jacob shall be in the midst of many people as a dew from the Lord, as the showers upon the grass, that tarrieth not for man, nor waiteth for the sons of men. And the remnant of Jacob shall be among the Gentiles in the midst of many people as a lion

74

among the beasts of the forest, as a young lion among the flocks of sheep: who, if he go through, both treadeth down, and teareth in pieces, and none can deliver. Thine hand shall be lifted up upon thine adversaries, and all thine enemies shall be cut off."

Hear the prophecy of Haggai 2:22: "I will overthrow the throne of kingdoms, and I will destroy the strength of the kingdoms of the heathen; and I will overthrow the chariots, and those that ride in them; and the horses and their riders shall come down, every one by the sword of his brother!"

Matthew's Gospel records a very enlightening passage concerning Christ's judgment of the nations, when the King shall say to those on His left hand, "Depart from me, ye cursed, into everlasting fire, prepared for the devil and his angels! For I was an hungred, and ye gave me no meat: I was thirsty, and ye gave me no drink: I was a stranger, and ye took me not in: naked, and ye clothed me not: sick, and in prison, and ye visited me not.

"Then shall they also answer Him, saying, Lord, when saw we thee an hungred, or athirst, or a stranger, or naked, or sick, or in prison, and did not minister unto thee? Then shall He answer them, saying, Verily, I say unto you, Inasmuch as ye did it not to one of the least of these, ye did it not to me. And these shall go away into everlasting punishment: but the righteous into life eternal" (Matt. 25:41—46).

7. *"In thee shall all families of the earth be blessed."* This great promise *has been,* is *being,* and *will be* fulfilled in the Lord Jesus Christ, God's only begotten Son. From the flesh side, Jesus came through the seed of Abraham. He has blessed, and is blessing, millions; but the greatest blessing is in the future when King Jesus sits on the throne of David in Jerusalem and reigns over this earth. Isaiah declares, "Unto us a Child is born, unto us a Son is given: and the government shall be upon His shoulder; and His name shall be called Wonderful, Counsellor, The mighty God, The everlasting Father, The Prince of Peace. *Of the increase of His government and peace there shall be no end, upon the throne of David, and upon His kingdom, to order it, and to establish it with judgment and with justice from henceforth even for ever.* The zeal of the Lord of hosts will perform this" (Isa. 9:6, 7). Isaiah penned these words seven hundred and fifty years before Christ was born; but He was born as prophesied, He was all Isaiah said He would be—"Wonderful, Counsellor, The Mighty God, the Everlasting Father, The Prince of Peace." He gave peace to all who would believe on Him and He is *still giving peace* to all who will believe! But there has never yet been "peace on earth, good will toward men." The government has not yet been laid on Christ's shoulders. These things are yet future—and just as surely as Jesus was born into this world nearly two

thousand years ago, *the government WILL BE upon His shoulder and there WILL BE universal peace.* The curse will be lifted and men will study war no more. This will come to pass when Jesus comes the second time, when He comes as King of kings and Lord of lords. He came the first time as a lamb, a babe in a manger; but when He comes the second time He will come as King, as the Lion of the tribe of Judah!

God not only gave Isaiah the prophecy concerning the *birth* of the King, He also gave him the prophecy concerning the *character and quality of the kingdom* over which the King will reign:

"There shall come forth a rod out of the stem of Jesse, and a Branch shall grow out of his roots: And the Spirit of the Lord shall rest upon Him, the spirit of wisdom and understanding, the spirit of counsel and might, the spirit of knowledge and of the fear of the Lord; and shall make Him of quick understanding in the fear of the Lord: and He shall not judge after the sight of His eyes, neither reprove after the hearing of His ears: but with righteousness shall He judge the poor, and reprove with equity for the meek of the earth: and He shall smite the earth with the rod of His mouth, and with the breath of His lips shall He slay the wicked. And righteousness shall be the girdle of His loins, and faithfulness the girdle of His reins.

"The wolf also shall dwell with the lamb, and

77

the leopard shall lie down with the kid; and the calf and the young lion and the fatling together; and a little child shall lead them. And the cow and the bear shall feed; their young ones shall lie down together: and the lion shall eat straw like the ox. And the sucking child shall play on the hole of the asp, and the weaned child shall put his hand on the cockatrice' den. They shall not hurt nor destroy in all my holy mountain: for the earth shall be full of the knowledge of the Lord, as the waters cover the sea" (Isa. 11:1—9).

The promise God made to Abraham and his seed, the same promise given to David concerning the kingdom, spoke of *an eternal, transfigured, human kingdom* (II Sam. 7:13). For such a kingdom there must be a King, even the Son of man who will come the second time to this earth to sit on the throne of David and reign from Jerusalem. The prophet Daniel spoke of the coming kingdom and described it in these words:

"I saw in the night visions, and behold, One like *the Son of man* came with the clouds of heaven, and came to the Ancient of days, and they brought Him near before Him, *and there was given Him dominion, and glory, and a kingdom, that all people, nations, and languages, should serve Him: His dominion is an everlasting dominion, which shall not pass away, and His kingdom that which shall not be destroyed"*

(Dan. 7:13, 14).

The Bodily Resurrection of Jesus
Guarantees the Millennium

Peter said to Jesus, "Behold, we have forsaken all, and followed thee. What shall we have therefore?" Jesus replied, "Verily I say unto you, That ye which have followed me, in the regeneration when the Son of man shall sit in the throne of His glory, ye also shall sit upon twelve thrones, judging the twelve tribes of Israel. And every one that hath forsaken houses, or brethren, or sisters, or father, or mother, or wife, or children, or lands, for my name's sake, shall receive an hundredfold, and shall inherit everlasting life" (Matt. 19:27—29).

In verse 28 of this passage the Greek word translated *"regeneration"* literally reads *"re-creation,"* or *"making new."* The same Greek word is used in Titus 3:5—"not by works of righteousness which we have done, but according to His mercy He saved us, *by the washing of REGENERATION, and renewing of the Holy Ghost."* In Titus, the passage speaks of the new birth that brings salvation to the soul. In Matthew, it speaks of the new birth of the earth, which is yet future. The glorious day is coming when the earth and *all creation* will be delivered from the pain, woe, and groaning it has been going through for six thousand years— since the day when Adam sinned. God did not intend for thorns to grow on this earth. He did

not intend for storms to sweep across the earth—
tornadoes, hurricanes, floods, thunder and lightning. These things are results of the curse. But
one day there will be no more groaning, no more
pain, no more sickness, sorrow, or death. Read
Isaiah chapter 11—*and believe it!* God will keep
His promise to David: "Incline your ear, and
come unto me: hear, and your soul shall live;
and I will make an *everlasting covenant with you,
even THE SURE MERCIES OF DAVID*" (Isa.
55:3).

On the Day of Pentecost, Peter preached to a
congregation gathered from every nation under
heaven at that time, and to that world-wide congregation he declared that the Seed of David would
one day be King as declared by the Old Testament
prophets. He said, "Men and brethren, let me
freely speak unto you of the patriarch David, that
he is both dead and buried, and his sepulchre is
with us unto this day. Therefore being a prophet,
and knowing that *God had sworn with an oath to
him, that of the fruit of his loins, according to the
flesh, He would raise up Christ to sit on his
throne;* he seeing this before spake of *the resurrection of Christ, that His soul was not left in hell,
neither His flesh did see corruption*"(Acts 2:29–31).

God swore with an oath to David that "the
fruit of his loins" (his seed) would sit on the
throne, and Peter named the Seed: *Christ, the
same Jesus* who died on the cross. "Therefore let

all the house of Israel know assuredly, that God hath made that same Jesus, whom ye have crucified, both Lord and Christ" (Acts 2:36). David, seeing that Jesus would sit on the throne in Jerusalem, spoke of the *resurrection* of Christ—the only possible way by which He *could* sit on the throne, for Peter was preaching on this side of the cross.

In Acts 15:13—18 James gave a clear blueprint of this present Day of Grace and of the kingdom on earth which is to follow. Before the council in Jerusalem he declared:

"Men and brethren, hearken unto me: Simeon hath declared how God at the first did *visit the Gentiles, to take out of them a people for His name.* And to this agree the words of the prophets; as it is written, *AFTER THIS I will return,* and will build again the tabernacle of David, which is fallen down; and I will build again the ruins thereof, and I will set it up: that the residue of men might seek after the Lord, and all the Gentiles, upon whom my name is called, saith the Lord, who doeth all these things. Known unto God are all His works from the beginning of the world."

Now what did James declare? First, God would visit the Gentiles to take out of them a people for His name. This has been going on since Pentecost and will continue until the Rapture of the Church. Then, after the judgment seat of Christ for believers

81

(during which time the tribulation period will run its course on earth), at the end of the tribulation *Jesus will return with His Church,* His bride, and the saints will reign with Him for one thousand glorious years of peace right here upon this earth. The tabernacle of David will be rebuilt in Jerusalem and that city will become the center of worship. When that time comes, the whole earth will be filled with the knowledge of the Lord as the waters now cover the sea.

The Spiritual Resurrection of Israel

Many people declare that God has finished with the Jew. They spiritualize the promises God made to Abraham and David, they take those promises and give them to the Church. They spiritualize the millennial kingdom, teaching that the Church will finally *convert the world* and bring in the kingdom. Such people are spiritual robbers. They wrongly divide the Word in order to defend a religion or a denomination, instead of studying to prove themselves approved unto God and *rightly* dividing the Word. But in spite of what men teach or preach, God *has not* finished with Israel, and that nation's most glorious days are yet to be! This is clearly set forth in Paul's letter to the Christians at Rome:

"I say then, Hath God cast away His people? God forbid! For I also am an Israelite, of the seed of Abraham, of the tribe of Benjamin. God hath not cast away His people which He foreknew. Wot ye not what the Scripture saith of Elias? How he maketh intercession to God against Israel, saying: *Lord, they have killed thy prophets, and digged down thine altars; and I am left alone, and they seek my life.*

"But what saith the answer of God unto him? *I have reserved to myself seven thousand men, who have not bowed the knee to the image of Baal!* Even so then at this present time also there is a remnant according to the election of grace. And if by grace, then it is no more of works: otherwise grace is no more grace. But if it be of works, then is it no more grace: otherwise work is no more work.

"What then? Israel hath not obtained that which he seeketh for; but the election hath obtained it, *and the rest were blinded* (according as it is written, God hath given them the spirit of slumber, eyes that they should not see, and ears that they should not hear) *unto this day.* And David saith, Let their table be made a snare, and a trap, and a stumblingblock, and a recompence unto them: Let their eyes be darkened, that they may not see, and bow down their back alway.

"I say then, Have they stumbled that they should fall? God forbid! but rather *through their fall* salvation is come unto *the Gentiles,* for to provoke them to jealousy. *Now if the FALL of them be the riches of the world, and the diminishing of them the riches of the Gentiles, how much MORE their fulness?* For I speak to you Gentiles, inasmuch as I am the apostle of the Gentiles, I magnify mine office: if by any means I may provoke to emulation them which are my flesh, and might save some of them.

"For if the *casting away* of them be the reconciling of the world, what shall the *receiving* of them be, but life from the dead? For if the firstfruit be holy, the lump is also holy: and if the root be holy, so are the branches. And if some of the branches be broken off, and thou, being a wild olive tree, wert graffed in among them, and with them partakest of the root and fatness of the olive tree, boast not against the branches. But if thou boast, thou bearest not the root, but the root thee.

"Thou wilt say then, The branches were broken off, that I might be graffed in. Well; *because of UNBELIEF they were broken off, and thou standest by FAITH.* Be not highminded, but fear: For if God spared not the natural branches, take heed lest He also spare not thee.

"Behold therefore the goodness and severity of God: On them which fell, severity; but toward thee, goodness, if thou continue in His goodness: otherwise thou also shalt be cut off. And they also, if they abide not still in unbelief, shall be graffed in: for God is able to graff them in again. For if thou wert cut out of the olive tree which is wild by nature, and wert graffed contrary to nature into a good olive tree: how much more shall these, which be the natural branches, be graffed into their own olive tree?

"For I would not, brethren, that ye should be ignorant of this mystery, lest ye should be wise in your own conceits; that *blindness in part is happened to Israel, until the fulness of the Gentiles be come in. And so ALL ISRAEL SHALL BE SAVED:* as it is written, There shall come out of Sion the Deliverer, and shall turn away ungodliness from Jacob: For this is my covenant unto them, when I shall take away their sins.

"As concerning the Gospel, they are enemies for your sakes: but as touching the election, they are beloved for the fathers' sakes. *For the gifts and calling of God are WITHOUT REPENTANCE.* For as ye in times past have not believed God, yet have now obtained mercy through their unbelief: even so have these also now not believed, that through your mercy they also may obtain mercy. For God hath concluded them all in unbelief, that He might have mercy upon all.

"O THE DEPTH OF THE RICHES BOTH OF THE WISDOM AND KNOWLEDGE OF GOD! How unsearchable are His judgments, and His ways past finding out! For who hath known the mind of the Lord? Or who hath been His counsellor? Or who hath first given to Him, and it shall be recompensed unto him again? *For of Him, and through Him, and to Him, are ALL THINGS:*

85

to whom be glory for ever. Amen" (Rom. 11:1—36).

Indeed *God has NOT turned His back on Israel* —nor will He ever do so! There always has been and always will be a faithful remnant of the Jewish people, until that day when *all Israel* shall be saved. At this present time there is, as Paul so emphatically declares, "a remnant *according to the election of grace,*" and since "the gifts and calling of God are without repentance" He has not repented concerning His promises to Abraham and David. The nation Israel will be resurrected spiritually, that nation will be born in a day, they will recognize their Messiah by the prints of the nails in His hands and feet, and they will love and worship Him as Lord and King.

The Prophet Ezekiel saw this in his vision of the valley of dry bones. His prophecy is both spiritual and physical:

"The hand of the Lord was upon me, and carried me out in the Spirit of the Lord, and set me down in the midst of the valley which was full of bones, and caused me to pass by them round about: and, behold, there were very many in the open valley; and, lo, they were very dry. And He said unto me, *Son of man, can these bones live?* And I answered, *O Lord God, thou knowest.*

"Again He said unto me, Prophesy upon these bones, and say unto them, *O ye dry bones, hear the Word of the Lord. Thus saith the Lord God unto these bones:* Behold, I will cause breath to enter into you, and ye shall live: and I will lay sinews upon you, and will bring up flesh upon you, and cover you with skin, and put breath in you, and ye shall live: and ye shall know that I am the Lord.

"So I prophesied as I was commanded: and as I prophesied, there was a noise, and behold a shaking, and the bones came together, bone to his bone. And when I beheld, lo, the sinews and the flesh came up upon them, and the skin covered them above: but there was no breath in them. Then said He unto me, Prophesy unto the wind, prophesy, son of man, and say to the wind, Thus saith the Lord God: Come from the four winds, O breath, and breathe upon these slain, that they may live.

"So I prophesied as He commanded me, and the breath came into them, and they lived, and stood up upon their feet, an exceeding great army. Then He said unto me, *Son of man, these bones are THE WHOLE HOUSE OF ISRAEL:* Behold, they say, Our bones are dried, and our hope is lost: we are cut off for our parts. Therefore prophesy and say unto them, Thus saith the Lord God: Behold, O my people, I will open your graves . . ." (This is descriptive language. The "graves" are nations of the world. Israel is buried *among* the people of other nations, and the "graves" here are not intended as *literal* graves.) ". . . and cause you to come up out of your graves, and bring you into the land of Israel. And ye shall know that I am the Lord, when I have opened your graves, O my people, and brought you up out of your graves, and shall put my Spirit in you, and ye shall live, and I shall place you in your own land. Then shall ye know that I the Lord have spoken it, and performed it, saith the Lord" (Ezek. 37:1—14).

The bones seen by Ezekiel represent the whole house of Israel. God promised to bring them back from throughout the nations where they have been buried (hidden) for twenty-five centuries. He will bring them back into their own land. Then when Jesus stands on the Mount of Olives (Zech. 14:4) at the end of the tribulation period, they will know Him as their Lord and God.

The greatest fulfillment of prophecy since the virgin birth of Jesus was the birth of the nation Israel in the month of May, 1948. For the first time in over two thousand years the Jews set up their own government, elected their own president, and were recognized as a nation among other nations. Today they are in their own land—in unbelief, of course—but their activity is setting the stage for the second coming of the Lord Jesus Christ.

I repeat—the best days for Israel are just ahead. They *will be* blessed as they have never been blessed before. They will prosper as never before. But all of this will take place when Jesus comes to them the second time, and *if He had remained in the grave* there could be no second coming!

The Prophet Isaiah saw this glorious day for Israel:

"For, behold, I create new heavens and a new earth." (This will be before the beginning of eternity.) "And the former shall not be remembered, nor come into mind. But be ye glad and rejoice for ever in that which I create: for, behold, I create Jerusalem a rejoicing and her people a joy." (The rejoicing will be twofold—during the thousand-year reign of Christ on earth, and also in the new earth.) "And I will rejoice in Jerusalem, and joy in my people: and the voice of weeping shall be no more heard in her, nor the voice of crying. There shall be no more thence an infant of days, nor an old man that hath not filled his days: for the child shall die an hundred years old; but the sinner being an hundred years old shall be accursed.

"And they shall build houses, and inhabit them; and they shall plant vineyards, and eat the fruit of them. They shall not build, and another inhabit; they shall not plant, and another eat: for as the days of a tree are the days of my people, and mine elect shall long enjoy the work of their hands. They shall not labour in vain, nor bring forth for trouble; for they are the seed of the blessed of the Lord, and their offspring with them. And it shall come to pass, that before they call, I will answer; and while they are yet speaking, I will hear. The wolf and the lamb shall feed together, and the lion shall eat straw like the bullock: and dust shall be the serpent's meat. They shall not hurt nor destroy in all my holy mountain, saith the Lord" (Isa. 65:17— 25). In connection with this Scripture please study Isaiah chapter 66.

At the beginning of the Millennium, the curse will be lifted from the earth (Isa. chapter 11), and Satan will be chained in hell for one thousand years:

"I saw an Angel come down from heaven, having the key of the bottomless pit and a great chain in His hand. And He laid hold on the dragon, that old serpent, which is the Devil, and Satan, and bound him a thousand years, and cast him into the bottomless pit, and shut him up, and set a seal upon him, that he should deceive the nations no more, till the thousand years should be fulfilled: and after that he must be loosed a little season" (Rev. 20:1—3).

Jesus will be on the throne in Jerusalem, and the saints will be with Him: "I saw thrones, and they sat upon them, and judgment was given unto them: and I saw the souls of them that were beheaded for the witness of Jesus, and for the Word of God, and which had not worshipped the beast, neither his image, neither had received his mark upon their foreheads, or in their hands; and they lived and reigned with Christ a thousand years. But the rest of the dead lived not again until the thousand years were finished. This is the first resurrection. Blessed and holy is he that hath part in the first resurrection: on such the second death hath no power, but they shall be priests of God and of Christ, and shall reign with Him a thousand years" (Rev. 20:4—6).

Dear reader, are YOU a believer? Do you know beyond any shadow of doubt that you are born again? If you are not sure of your salvation, do not spend another moment in unbelief! Give your heart to Jesus now, He will save you, and you will know it. Then you will have a part in the glorious days that are ahead for all born again believers!

The Bodily Resurrection of Jesus
Guarantees the Spiritual New Birth of the Nations

Not only will the nation of *Israel* be blessed exceedingly in the Kingdom of Heaven on earth, but the nations who are *friendly toward Israel* during the reign of Antichrist will be blessed also, along with the nations which will be saved through the preaching of the 144,000 Jewish missionaries sealed out of the twelve tribes of Israel. (In connection with this, please read Revelation chapter 7.)

All creation is under the curse and will remain so until the Millennium. The only peace in this earth today is in the hearts of individuals who know the Lord and who are fully surrendered to Him. The Prophet Isaiah declares, "Thou wilt keep him in perfect peace, whose mind is stayed on thee: because he trusteth in thee'' (Isa. 26:3). We live in a world that is cursed because of man's sin; but one glorious day the curse will be lifted and this earth and its inhabitants will know peace and serenity. Think of all the misery in the world at this moment—bloodshed, pain, sorrow, sickness, hunger, turmoil, strife, hatred—all because of sin! But one day this tragic state of affairs will come to an end *and peace will reign supreme!*

For example, Egypt and Assyria (as nations) have never been God's people. They have never been at peace with God. But hear the words of Isaiah concerning those two nations in the future:

''The Lord *shall be* known to Egypt, and the Egyptians shall know the Lord in that day, and shall do sacrifice and oblation; yea, they shall vow a vow unto the Lord, and perform it. And the Lord shall smite Egypt: He shall smite and heal it: and they shall return even to the Lord, and He shall be intreated of them, and shall heal them.

''In that day shall there be a highway out of Egypt to Assyria, and the Assyrian shall come into Egypt, and the Egyptian into Assyria, and the Egyptians shall serve with the Assyrians. In that day shall Israel be the third with Egypt and with Assyria, even a blessing in the midst of the land: whom the Lord of hosts shall bless, saying, *Blessed be Egypt my people, and Assyria the work of my hands, and ISRAEL MINE INHERITANCE''* (Isa. 19:21—25).

In Isaiah 25:8 we read, *"He* (God) *will swallow up death in victory; and the Lord God will wipe away tears from off all faces; and the rebuke of His people shall He take away from off all the earth: FOR THE LORD HATH SPOKEN IT."*

The Bodily Resurrection of Jesus Guarantees That All Nature Will Experience A New Birth

Yes, one day there will be a rebirth of all nature—no more thorns, thistles, or briars, no more destructive killing among members of the animal kingdom—"the wolf also shall dwell with the lamb, and the leopard shall lie down with the kid; and the calf and the young lion and the fatling together; and a little child shall lead them. And the cow and the bear shall feed; their young ones shall lie down together: and the lion shall eat straw like the ox. And the sucking child shall play on the hole of the asp, and the weaned child shall put his hand on the cockatrice' den" (Isa. 11:6—8). As in the days of Adam and Noah, men will live to be hundreds of years old: "There shall be no more thence an infant of days, nor an old man that hath not filled his days: for the child shall die an hundred years old; but the sinner being an hundred years old shall be accursed" (Isa. 65:20).

All of these glorious things are *divinely guaranteed* because of Christ's victory over the world, the flesh, the devil, death, hell, and the grave.

He lives now at the right hand of God, but one day He will return to this earth to reign in righteousness. Today there is a Man in heaven, the Man who rose bodily from the tomb, the Man Christ Jesus, our soon coming King. At the appointed time He will return to this earth, and He will deliver the entire creation from the curse. Satan will be placed in the bottomless pit along with the beast, the false prophet, and all of the wicked. Then there will be peace on earth, good will toward men. All things will be made new, for the former things will have passed away. There will be no more sorrow, no more dying, no more sickness or pain. There will be one eternal day of peace and glory with Jesus!

The Bodily Resurrection of Jesus
Guarantees A New Heaven, A New Earth,
And the Pearly White City

"And I saw a new heaven and a new earth: for the first heaven and the first earth were passed away; and there was no more sea. And I John saw the holy city, new Jerusalem, coming down from God out of heaven, prepared as a bride adorned for her husband. And I heard a great voice out of heaven saying: Behold, the tabernacle of God is with men, and He will dwell with them, and they shall be His people, and God Himself shall be with them, and be their God. And God shall wipe away all tears from their eyes; and there shall be no more death, neither sorrow, nor crying, neither shall there be any more pain: for the former things are passed away.

"And He that sat upon the throne said, *Behold, I make all things NEW*. And He said unto me, *Write: for these words are true and faithful*. And He said unto me, *It is done. I AM ALPHA AND OMEGA, the beginning and the end*. I will give unto him that is athirst of the fountain of the water of life freely. He that overcometh shall inherit all things; and I will be his God, and he shall be my son. But the fearful, and unbelieving, and the abominable, and murderers, and whoremongers, and sorcerers, and idolaters, and all liars, shall have their part in the lake which burneth with fire and brimstone: which is the second death.

"And there came unto me one of the seven angels which had the seven vials full of the seven last plagues, and talked with me, saying, *Come hither, I will shew thee the bride, the Lamb's wife*. And he carried me away in the Spirit to a great and high mountain, and shewed me that great city, the holy Jerusalem, descending out of heaven from God, having the glory of God: and her light was like unto a stone most precious, even like a jasper stone, clear as crystal; and had a wall great and high, and had twelve gates, and at the gates twelve angels, and names written thereon, which are the names of the twelve tribes of the children of Israel. On the east three gates; on the north three gates; on the south three gates; and on the west three gates. And the wall of the city had twelve foundations, and in them the names of the twelve apostles of the Lamb.

"And he that talked with me had a golden reed to measure the city, and the gates thereof, and the wall thereof. And the city lieth foursquare, and the length is as large as the breadth: and he measured the city with the reed, twelve thousand furlongs. The length and the breadth and the height of it are equal. And he measured the wall thereof, an hundred and forty and four cubits, according to the measure of a man, that is, of the angel. And the building of the wall of it was of jasper: and the city was pure gold, like unto clear glass.

"And the foundations of the wall of the city were garnished with all manner of precious stones. The first foundation was jasper; the second, sapphire; the third, a chalcedony; the fourth, an emerald; the fifth, sardonyx; the sixth, sardius; the seventh, chrysolyte; the eighth, beryl; the ninth, a topaz; the tenth, a chrysoprasus; the eleventh, a jacinth; the twelfth, an amethyst. And the twelve gates were twelve pearls; every several gate was of one pearl: and the street of the city was pure gold, as it were transparent glass.

"And I saw no temple therein: for the Lord God Almighty and the Lamb are the temple of it.

96

And the city had no need of the sun, neither of the moon, to shine in it: for the glory of God did lighten it, and the Lamb is the light thereof. And the nations of them which are saved shall walk in the light of it: and the kings of the earth do bring their glory and honour into it. And the gates of it shall not be shut at all by day: for there shall be no night there. And they shall bring the glory and honour of the nations into it. And there shall in no wise enter into it any thing that defileth, neither whatsoever worketh abomination, or maketh a lie: but they which are written in the Lamb's book of life.

"And he shewed me a pure river of water of life, clear as crystal, proceeding out of the throne of God and of the Lamb. In the midst of the street of it, and on either side of the river, was there the tree of life, which bare twelve manner of fruits, and yielded her fruit every month: and the leaves of the tree were for the healing of the nations.

"And there shall be no more curse: but the throne of God and of the Lamb shall be in it; and His servants shall serve Him: and they shall see His face; and His name shall be in their foreheads. And there shall be no night there; and they need no candle, neither light of the sun; for the Lord God giveth them light: and they shall reign for ever and ever.

"And he said unto me, These sayings are faithful

and true: and the Lord God of the holy prophets sent His angel to shew unto His servants the things which must *shortly* be done. *BEHOLD, I COME QUICKLY!* Blessed is he that keepeth the sayings of the prophecy of this book" (Rev. 21:1—22:7).

We have already discussed the Millennium— the thousand-year reign of Christ on earth, an era more glorious than anything this earth has ever known. But the Millennium is only *the beginning* of "all things made new."

There will be thousands upon thousands of babies born *during* the millennial reign of Christ, and since Satan will be chained in hell throughout that time these children will grow up without having known temptation. Also there will be a multitude of people who will give lip-service to King Jesus but will not give heart-service. These people must all be put to the test. Therefore at the close of the Millennium Satan will be loosed for a little season, and he will put those people to the test just as he did Adam and Eve and all others up to the beginning of the Millennium. Some will listen to him, others will choose to follow Jesus. Those who *do* follow Satan will make up the great army which will forge the last all-out attempt to destroy the *city of God* and the *people* of God. This will be the battle of Gog and Magog, as described in Revelation 20:7—9:

"And when the thousand years are expired, Satan shall be loosed out of his prison, and shall go out to deceive the nations which are in the four quarters of the earth, Gog and Magog, to gather them together to battle: the number of whom is as the sand of the sea. And they went up on the breadth of the earth, and compassed the camp of the saints about, and the beloved city: *and fire came down from God out of heaven, AND DEVOURED THEM!*"

(This is *definitely NOT* the battle of Armageddon which is to be fought at the close of the Great Tribulation, as described in Revelation 14:14—20 when blood will run to the horses' bridles for the space of "a thousand and six hundred furlongs"— or about 200 miles. The battle of Armageddon will be fought in the Valley of Armageddon *just outside Jerusalem,* but the battle of Gog and Magog will be fought *around and IN* the beloved city.)

In the battle of Gog and Magog, Jerusalem will be completely surrounded by the enemy—an army "the number of whom is *as the sand of the sea.*" Think of it! Who could begin to number the sand of the sea? But when this great army has the Holy City completely surrounded, when it seems as if the city and its inhabitants (including the saints of God) will be annihilated, fire will come down from heaven and devour the enemy! God will fight this battle with FIRE—God deals in fire and blood.

Immediately after this great battle of Gog and

Magog, Satan will be cast into the lake of fire and brimstone to remain there forever, never again to deceive mankind. After this, the unbelieving dead will be judged and they, too, will be cast into the lake that burns with fire and brimstone (Rev. 20: 11–15). Then, when all evil and all wicked ones are in the pit, the eternity of eternities will begin! There will be new heavens, a new earth, and the Pearly White City, just as John saw it "in the Spirit on the Lord's Day" (Rev. 1:10). *We* will see it *literally,* and we will live in the midst of "all things made new."

In that glorious day, soul, spirit, and body will be glorified. The redeemed will have a body like the glorious resurrection body of Jesus (I John 3:2). *All nature and matter* will be completely transfigured, created new. The curse will be completely removed and neither heaven nor earth will bear one trace of sin! The Pearly White City (eternal home of the New Testament Church) will be beyond description in terms of human language, for the finite mind of man cannot think or imagine the splendor and glories of the city John saw descending from God out of heaven! We will appreciate these glories only when we stand in the presence of our glorified Lord, when we ourselves are clothed in our glorified bodies.

The bodily resurrection of Jesus is God's guarantee that all things *will be* created new. *Matter* was transfigured for the first time when Jesus came from the tomb—*Christ, the firstfruits.* When He, in His resurrection body, first appeared to ten of the disciples (Thomas was not present) they were terrified—they thought they were seeing the *ghost* of their Lord. But Jesus said to them, *"Behold my hands and my feet, that it is I myself. Handle me, and see; for a spirit hath not flesh and bones, as ye see me have"* (Luke 24:36—39). The nailprints were still visible in His hands and feet, the print of the Roman spear was still visible in His side, as revealed to Thomas in John 20: 26—28.

The bodily resurrection of Jesus assures us that matter is *capable* of transfiguration, and in God's appointed time all matter *will be* transfigured. Jesus is not only the firstfruits of them that sleep, He is the firstfruits of all things created new, all things transfigured. Without His *bodily resurrection* there would be no new heaven, no new earth, no Pearly White City—and there could be no peace on earth, no good will among men. *Our* bodily resurrection from the grave, the transfiguration of the heavens and the earth, all things created new— these depend entirely upon the bodily resurrection of the Lord Jesus Christ.

He came to redeem—*to buy back*—all that Adam lost in the fall. He finished that which He came to do (John 19:30) and because of His finished work we have the divine guarantee that believers, too, will be raised incorruptible and there will be a new creation—completely free from sin and from the curse. The final results of His bodily resurrection are declared in Isaiah 65:17: "Behold, I create new heavens and a new earth: *and the former shall not be remembered, nor come into mind!*"

Christ's bodily resurrection is the substance of all the promises of God, from Adam through the transfiguration of all things—the fulfillment of God's promises to the fathers, the fulfillment of *ALL of God's promises* from Genesis 3:15 until the eternity of eternities begins. In Luke 24:44, Jesus (in His resurrection body) endorsed the promises of God. He said, "These are the words which I spake unto you, while I was yet with you, that *all things must be fulfilled, which were written in the law of Moses, and in the prophets and in the Psalms, concerning me.*" Without Christ's bodily resurrection, God could not have *kept* His promises.

But every promise God has made will be fulfilled completely and to the letter. The bodily resurrection of His only begotten Son guarantees that the heavenly Father will keep His promise concerning *all who are sons through faith in the finished work of Jesus.*

"He is not here—HE IS RISEN!" Not only do these seven words declare more truth than any other seven words in the Bible—they also declare *truth that makes ALL Bible truth TRUTH.* If the devil |could have prevented the bodily resur-

rection of Jesus, we would have no Bible, we would have no salvation, we would have no hope, because the bodily resurrection of the only begotten Son of God is the heart, blood-stream, life and soul of our Bible. It is the visible display of the exceeding greatness of God's power to us-ward—yea, to everyone who is a believer, whether asleep in Jesus or alive on earth.

To His disciples Jesus declared, "Yet a little while, and the world seeth me no more. *But YE see me:* because *I* live, *YE shall live also*" (John 14:19).

The Apostle Paul explained, "If Christ be in you, the *body* is dead because of sin; but the *Spirit is LIFE* because of righteousness" (Rom. 8:10).

Dear friend, if you are a believer, how long has it been since you bowed your head and sincerely thanked God for Jesus—for His life, death, burial, and resurrection? How long has it been since you worshipped God in prayer, thanking Him for the divine truth that at this very moment the Man Christ Jesus is seated at the right hand of the Majesty, making intercession for you? How long has it been since you praised God and thanked Him for His mercy and love—without *asking* Him for anything? It was God who gave Jesus to die on the cross for our sins, literally turning His back on His dear Son as He "bare our sins in His own body on the tree" (I Pet. 2:24,

25).   Paul said, *"We also JOY IN GOD through our Lord Jesus Christ,* by whom we have now received the atonement"* (Rom. 5:11).   How long has it been since you bowed in prayer and found *real JOY* in praising God in thanksgiving, thanking Him for all the blessings He has showered upon you since He saved you?   "Every good gift and every perfect gift is from above, and cometh down from the Father of lights, with whom is no variableness, neither shadow of turning" (James 1:17).

Dear sinner friend, will *you* please think seriously about your eternal welfare?   Where will *you* spend eternity?   If you spend it in hell it will be by your own choice, for God is not willing that you perish, He would that you repent and be saved: "The Lord is not . . . willing that *any* should perish, but that *all* should come to repentance" (II Pet. 3:9).

God has no pleasure in the death of the wicked, it is His joy to save all who will come to Him in the name of Jesus.   Won't you bow your head, confess your sin, and ask Jesus to come into your heart this moment?   He will save you, and then you, too, can "joy in God," rejoicing that your name is written in the Lamb's book of life!

SEVEN THINGS OF GOD

Seven Things of God

"That which was from the beginning, which we have heard, which we have seen with our eyes, which we have looked upon, and our hands have handled, of the Word of life; (for the life was manifested, and we have seen it, and bear witness, and shew unto you that eternal life, which was with the Father, and was manifested unto us;) That which we have seen and heard declare we unto you, that ye also may have fellowship with us: and truly our fellowship is with the Father and with His Son Jesus Christ.

"And these things write we unto you, that your joy may be full. This then is the message which we have heard of Him, and declare unto you, that God is light, and in Him is no darkness at all. If we say that we have fellowship with Him, and walk in darkness, we lie, and do not the truth: but if we walk in the light, as He is in the light, we have fellowship one with another, and the blood of Jesus Christ His Son cleanseth us from all sin.

"If we say that we have no sin, we deceive ourselves, and the truth is not in us. If we confess our sins, He is faithful and just to forgive us our sins, and to cleanse us from all unrighteousness. If we say that we have not sinned, we make Him a liar, and His Word is not in us" (I John 1:1—10).

Most outstanding Bible scholars agree that John's writings—his Gospel, his three epistles, and The Revelation—contain God's last message to man. The Gospel of John is said to have been written about 85 or 90 A. D., his three epistles in 90 A. D., and The Revelation in 96 A. D. The student of God's Word will readily see that there is a sequence of thought—and a world of suggestion—in these dates.

The Gospel of John carries us back to the eternity behind us: *"In the beginning* was the Word, and the Word was with God, and the Word was God"* (John 1:1).

The key to the Epistles of John hangs at the very front door, and it is impossible to miss the message of these writings: "These things write we unto you, that your joy may be full" (I John 1:4). Thus the epistles lead us into this present life. In them we find strength for the day. In them we find assurance, joy, and guaranteed victory through Christ.

As we read John's first epistle we soon realize that we are reading a Father's love-letter to His children. God is the Father, and we who are born again are the children. John uses two Greek words for "children." *Teknon* means "an offspring," and it is true that we are the offspring of God, we are born of God (John 1:12,13; I John 3:1). The second

Greek word, *teknion,* is even dearer. It is a tender, endearing word denoting close fellowship and deep love. This word is used seven times in the first epistle of John:

I John 2:1, 12, 28: *"My little children,* these things write I unto you, that ye sin not, And if any man sin, we have an Advocate with the Father, Jesus Christ the righteous: . . . I write unto you, *little children,* because your sins are forgiven you for His name's sake. . . . And now, *little children,* abide in Him; that, when He shall appear, we may have confidence, and not be ashamed before Him at His coming."

I John 3:7, 18: *"Little children,* let no man deceive you: he that doeth righteousness is righteous, even as HE is righteous. . . . *My little children,* let us not love in word, neither in tongue; but in deed and in truth."

I John 4:4: "Ye are of God, *little children,* and have overcome them: because greater is He that is in you, than he that is in the world."

I John 5:21: *"Little children,* keep yourselves from idols. Amen."

Thus the Greek word *teknion* makes these statements very paternal.

The Revelation, given to John on the Isle of Patmos, unfolds the glory of the future. John was commanded, "Write the things which thou *hast seen,* and the things which *are,* and the things which *shall be hereafter"* (Rev. 1:19). After John had seen these things, he wrote, "These sayings are faithful and true: and the Lord God of the holy prophets sent His angel to shew unto His servants *the things which must shortly be done"*(Rev. 22:6).

The Gospel of John was written "that (we) might believe that Jesus is the Christ, the Son of God; and that believing (we) might have life through His name" (John 20:31).

The Epistles of John were written that we who have believed unto eternal life might also have *full joy* (I John 1:4), which is the spiritual birthright of every believer.

The Revelation was given that we might have assurance of things which are to come to pass "shortly."

No wonder John is known as "the disciple whom Jesus loved"—John the Beloved. Some of the most endearing words in our Bible were penned by him, under inspiration of the Holy Spirit and by the direct revelation of God.

Error and heresy have existed in every period since the beginning of the human race. In John's time the pernicious error of Gnosticism held sway. The Gnostics taught that Christ did not *actually* come into the world, born of the Virgin Mary, but that He only *seemed* to do so, that He did not die *in reality* but *in appearance only.* Such doctrine constituted a denial of God in the flesh in the Person of the Lord Jesus Christ. Hence John's cutting words concerning those who were *deceivers,* "who confess not that *Jesus Christ is come IN THE FLESH.* This is a deceiver and an antichrist" (II John 7).

These false teachers of John's day—like the agnostics of today—taught that it is not possible to know positively whether there is a God, or a life beyond the grave. Thus John's many clear statements about *knowing.* Two Greek words used in John's epistles are translated *"know"*—one word means the knowledge of *perception,* the other means the knowledge of *personal acquaintance.*

Looking back into the past, John frequently says to the "little born ones," "You *have known"* —as in I John 2:13, 14: "I write unto you, fathers, because *ye have known HIM* that is from the beginning. I write unto you, young men, because ye have overcome the wicked one. I write unto you, little children, because *ye have known the Father.* I have written unto you, fathers, because *ye have known HIM* that is from the beginning. I have written unto you, young men, because ye are strong, and the Word of God abideth in you, and ye have overcome the wicked one."

In I John 4:16 John testifies, "We have *known and believed* the love that God hath to us. God is love; and he that dwelleth in love dwelleth in God, and God in him."

Emphasizing the present, John says, "Ye have an unction from the Holy One, and *YE KNOW all things.* I have not written unto you because ye

111

know *not* the truth, but *because YE KNOW IT,* and that no lie is of the truth. . . . If ye know that He is righteous, *YE KNOW that every one that do-eth righteousness is born of Him"* (I John 2:20,21,29).

"YE KNOW that He was manifested to take away our sins; and in Him is no sin. . . . Whosoever hateth his brother is a murderer: and *YE KNOW that no murderer* hath eternal life abiding in him" (I John 3:5, 15).

John includes himself in "knowing": "Hereby *we* do know that *we* know Him, if *we* keep His commandments. . . . Whoso keepeth His Word, in him verily is the love of God perfected: hereby know *we* that *we* are in Him. . . . Little children, it is the last time: and as ye have heard that anti-christ shall come, even now are there many anti-christs; *whereby WE KNOW that it is the last time"* (I John 2:3, 5, 18).

"Beloved, now are we the sons of God, and it doth not yet appear what we shall be: but *WE KNOW that, when He shall appear, we shall be like Him;* for *we* shall see Him as He is. . . . *WE KNOW that we have passed from death unto life,* because *we* love the brethren. He that loveth not his brother abideth in death. . . . Hereby *WE KNOW that we are of the truth,* and shall assure our hearts before Him. . . . He that keepeth His commandments dwelleth in Him, and He in him. And hereby *WE KNOW that He abideth in us,* by the Spirit which He hath given us" (I John 3:2,14,19,24).

"If *we know* that He hear us, whatsoever *we* ask, *WE KNOW that we have the petitions that we desired of Him....WE KNOW that whosoever is born of God sinneth not;* but he that is begotten of God keepeth himself, and that wicked one toucheth him not" (I John 5:15, 18).

To *emphasize* the fact of "knowing" John says, *"HEREBY we know"*—i. e., *"HEREBY know ye* the Spirit of God: Every spirit that confesseth that Jesus Christ is come in the flesh is of God:...We are of God: he that knoweth God heareth us; he that is not of God heareth not us. *HEREBY know we* the Spirit of truth, and the spirit of error. . . . *HEREBY know we* that we dwell in Him, and He in us, because He hath given us of His Spirit" (I John 4:2, 6, 13).

Speaking problematically John writes, *"IF ye know* that He is righteous, ye know that every one that doeth righteousness is born of Him" (I John 2:29).

In other places he explains, *"That we MAY know"*—as in I John 5:13, 20: "These things have I written unto you that believe on the name of the Son of God; *that YE MAY KNOW that ye have eternal life,* and that ye may believe on the name of the Son of God. . . . And we know that the Son of God is come, and hath given us an understanding, *that we MAY KNOW Him that is true,* and we are in Him that is true, even in His Son, Jesus Christ. This is the true God, and eternal life."

113

Thus the intent of the Holy Spirit is crystal-clear: It is that the "little children" of God need not live in doubt or fear, but that we possess the *enjoyment of KNOWING* the things of God. Christianity is not a question mark, it is *an exclamation point!* The great words in the Epistles of John are "LIFE...LIGHT... and LOVE." In the first epistle we find "Seven Things of God" which I wish to point out and discuss in this message.

I
The Word of God Is the Basis For All Authority

"I have written unto you, fathers, because ye have known Him that is from the beginning. I have written unto you, young men, because ye are strong, and the Word of God abideth in you, and ye have overcome the wicked one" (I John 2:14).

John writes to the "fathers" because they have known "Him that was from the beginning." He writes to the "young men" because the Word of God abides in them, giving them strength to overcome "the wicked one." *EVERYTHING depends upon THE WORD!*

Of whom does this verse speak? Who was it the fathers knew? They knew "Him that was from the beginning," and Genesis 1:1 identifies this Person: *"In the beginning GOD created...."* John 1:1, 2 gives further identification: *"In the beginning was THE WORD,* and the Word was *with* God, and the Word *was* God. The same was in the beginning *with* God."

With what authority do I preach God's love for sinners? With what authority do I declare that He will save all who call upon His name, believing in the finished work of His only begotten Son? With what authority do I declare that God is a God of love, that He loves even those who have sinned against Him? For that matter, with what authority do I declare in this message that *the Word of God is the BASIS of all authority?*

The BIBLE, the infallible, unalterable *WORD OF GOD* is the basis of my authority. Before the world was, before man was, before *anything* was that is, *THE WORD was with God!* The Psalmist declared, "Lord, thou hast been our dwelling place in all generations. Before the mountains were brought forth, or ever thou hadst formed the earth and the world, even *from everlasting to everlasting, thou art GOD"* (Psalm 90:1, 2).

The Word of God tells me that God loved man before his creation, and since God is omniscient, knowing the end from the beginning, He knew man would fall. Therefore, even before He *created* man, God perfected salvation. Peter declares, "Ye know that ye were not redeemed with corruptible things, as silver and gold . . . but with the precious blood of Christ, as of a lamb without blemish and without spot: who verily was *foreordained BEFORE THE FOUNDATION OF THE WORLD,* but was *manifest* in these last times for you" (I Pet. 1:18—20).

I know all of this is beyond human understanding. It is *by faith* that we believe, even though we do not understand (Heb. 11:3). I am so thankful that it *is* by faith and not by my own wisdom. If I could understand God, I would be as *wise* as God, and I am thankful that my God is greater and wiser than I! The fact that I cannot understand Him causes me to have more faith in Him and trust Him more.

One does not need an abundance of common sense to know that this creation did not just *"happen."* Therefore, since I know creation did not just happen, I know there is a Supreme Being. I know that *God IS*, and that *God DOES*. Also, I know there is a God because His Word tells me so —*"In the beginning GOD...."* But another reason I know there is a God is because more than a quarter of a century ago He changed my life completely—inside and out. I was raised in a Christian home. My good mother spent many sleepless nights because of my drinking and wickedness, and my father did all he could do to get me to change my way of living—but to no avail.

Then one night I stood in the doorway of a little country church and heard a minister deliver a message on Romans 6:23: *"The wages of SIN is DEATH;* but the gift of God is eternal life through Jesus Christ our Lord!"* I listened to what he said about dying in sin and spending eternity in hell, and then I listened to what he said about the gift of God—eternal life through faith in Jesus. At the close of his sermon I went forward and asked him to pray for me. I did not stay for prayer, but after everyone else had left the church I went back inside to talk with him. He knew I was lost, he knew I was under deep conviction. He took his little New Testament from his pocket and read John 3:16 aloud, then asked me if I believed it. I told him I had *always* believed the Bible. He said, "You have believed it in your *mind*, but not in your *heart*." He then explained to me that heart-belief meant trust, and asked me if I would trust Jesus to save my soul. He asked me if I sincerely *wanted* to be saved, if I sincerely believed that Jesus died for my sins, that He was buried, and that He rose again the third day as the Bible tells us He did. I assured him that I did believe these truths insofar as I *knew how* to believe. God knew I was sincere, He saved me that very moment, and I have never been the same since! God made a new creature of me—and it happened through His Living Word.

These are the verses that changed my whole life: "For God so loved the world that He gave His only begotten Son, that whosoever believeth in Him should not perish, but have everlasting life" (John 3:16). "If thou shalt confess with thy mouth the Lord Jesus, and shalt believe in thine heart that God hath raised Him from the dead, thou shalt be saved. For with the heart man believeth unto righteousness; and with the mouth confession is made unto salvation" (Rom. 10:9, 10).

Anyone who will receive the truth of these three verses will be saved and created anew in Christ Jesus: "Therefore if any man be in Christ, he is a new creature: old things are passed away; behold, all things are become new" (II Cor. 5:17).

God Loves All Men: —

"For God so *loved THE WORLD*... that *WHOSOEVER believeth*" might have eternal life (John 3:16). "God sent... His Son... *that THE WORLD through Him* might be saved" (John 3:17). "Come unto me *ALL YE that labour and are heavy laden* ..." (Matt. 11:28). "The Lord is not... willing *that ANY should perish,* but that *ALL* should come to repentance" (II Pet. 3:9).

There are many more verses in God's Word which clearly teach God's love for *all mankind;* but anyone who refuses to believe these verses I have given would not believe if I gave a hundred more! I speak with authority—the authority of God's infallible Word—when I declare that God loves you, and *you,* and *YOU.* He loves *ALL peoples of this earth,* regardless of race, creed, or social standing.

The One Way of Salvation: —

I also speak with authority when I declare that there is *only ONE WAY of salvation.* There are hundreds of "religions" but there is only one way of salvation—*the BIBLE WAY.* Jesus declared to

118

His disciples: "I am the WAY, the TRUTH, and the LIFE! *NO MAN cometh unto the Father but BY ME*" (John 14:6).

That settles it! When I declare from the pulpit or from the printed page that Jesus is the only way to heaven, the only way of salvation, I speak with authority because I speak the words of Jesus. To the religionists of His day He declared:

"Verily, verily, I say unto you, Except ye eat the flesh of the Son of man, and drink His blood, *ye have NO LIFE in you.* Whoso eateth my flesh, and drinketh my blood, hath eternal life; and I will raise him up at the last day. For my flesh is meat indeed, and my blood is drink indeed. He that eateth my flesh, and drinketh my blood, dwelleth in me, and I in him.... The WORDS that I speak unto you, they are spirit, and they are life" (John 6:53—56, 63).

It is the *Word of God* that opens the heart *(the inner man)* to the *desire for* salvation and the *"how"* of salvation. The entrance of the Word gives light, "it giveth understanding unto the simple" (Psalm 119:130). *Without light* there could be *no LIFE.* Light *brings* life, and light *sustains* life. Light is the sum of all knowledge, and the knowledge of salvation comes through the Word of God.

It is through the Word that we learn, *"ALL have sinned,* and come short of the glory of God" (Rom. 3:23). *"ALL we* like sheep have gone astray"

(Isa. 53:6). It is through the Word that we learn that *the GRACE OF GOD brings salvation* (Tit. 2:11), and *"BY GRACE are ye saved through FAITH;* and that not of yourselves: it is THE GIFT OF GOD"* (Eph. 2:8). Salvation becomes ours by faith—but *faith* comes only *through hearing the Word of God* (Rom. 10:17).

Jesus emphatically declared, *"Ye MUST be born again!"* (John 3:7). Apart from the new birth no one can enter heaven, and *apart from the Word of God* no one can be born again: We are born again "not of corruptible seed, but of incorruptible, by *the Word of God,* which liveth and abideth for ever" (I Pet. 1:23). James declares that we are begotten "with the Word of Truth..., the engrafted Word, which is able to save (our) souls" (James 1:18, 21).

The Psalmist declares, "Salvation belongeth unto the LORD" (Psalm 3:8), and Jonah repeats, "Salvation is of the Lord" (Jonah 2:9).

Paul explains that salvation is the Lord Jesus in the heart by faith—"Christ in you, the hope of glory" (Col. 1:27).

The Word of God warns, "There is a way that seemeth right unto a man, but the end thereof are the *ways of death"* (Prov. 16:25). Yes, there are many, many *"ways,"* but there is only ONE right Way—the *Jesus* way. All "ways" lead to destruction. The *one WAY* leads to life everlasting.

I also declare, on the authority of God's Word,

that born again believers can live a victorious life in the midst of sinful men, in the midst of a "crooked and perverse generation." God's Word plainly says, "Whosoever believeth that Jesus is the Christ is born of God, *and . . . whatsoever is born of God OVERCOMETH THE WORLD:* and this is the victory that overcometh the world, *even our FAITH*" (I John 5:1, 4). *"Whosoever"* includes all and excludes none. But notice: "Whosoever is BORN OF GOD"—not just a church member, not just a religionist, but saved by grace, washed in the blood, a new creation in Christ.

And what IS the victory that overcomes the world? *"Even our FAITH."* And the only way to have faith is through the Word of God. So again— "Faith cometh by hearing, and hearing by the Word of God" (Rom. 10:17). We *walk* by the same faith that saves us—"as it is written, *The just shall LIVE by faith*" (Rom. 1:17), and *"whatsoever is NOT of faith is sin"* (Rom. 14:23).

No wonder Satan has done—and is doing—all he can to discredit the Word of God. If he could prove the Word of God untrue he could undermine Christianity and send all mankind to the lowest hell! But we can declare with the Psalmist, *"For ever, O Lord, thy Word is SETTLED IN HEAVEN"* (Psalm 119:89). The liberals and modernists may offer new "versions" of the Bible, but that does not change *"Thus saith the LORD!"* Furthermore, "it is contained in the Scripture, Behold, I lay in Sion a Chief Cornerstone, elect, precious: and *he that believeth on HIM shall not be confounded* (confused)" (I Pet. 2:6).

II
The Love of God Is the Secret of All Godliness

"Whoso keepeth His Word, in him verily is *the LOVE OF GOD perfected:* hereby know we that we are in Him" (I John 2:5).

"He that loveth not knoweth not God; for *God IS love.* In this was manifested the love of God toward us, because that God sent His only begotten Son into the world, that we might live through Him. Herein is love, not that we loved God, but that *He loved us,* and sent His Son to be the propitiation for our sins. Beloved, if God so loved us, we ought also to love one another. No man hath seen God at any time. If we love one another, God dwelleth in us, and His love is perfected in us" (I John 4:8—12).

Only the love of God within the heart of an individual can change ungodly men and make them godly. Paul tells us that before the love of God appeared, we—yes, even believers—were "foolish, disobedient, deceived, serving divers lusts and pleasures, living in malice and envy, hateful, and hating one another. *But AFTER that the kindness and LOVE OF GOD OUR SAVIOUR toward man appeared,* not by works of righteousness which we have done, but according to His mercy He saved us, by the washing of regeneration, and renewing of the Holy Ghost; which He shed on us abundantly through Jesus Christ our Saviour" (Tit. 3:3—6).

"The kindness and love of God our Saviour" makes the difference. Godly people are godly because they know God our Saviour and the love of God abides within their hearts. This puts within the believer "the fruit of the Spirit...love, joy, peace, longsuffering, gentleness, goodness, faith, meekness, temperance: against such there is no law" (Gal. 5:22, 23).

It is wonderful to thank God for saving our soul, and for all the wonderful things He does for us day by day since we have been saved; but we should begin by thanking Him for *His love!* Remember—Jesus is our Saviour only because God loved us while we were very unlovable:

"When we were yet *without strength,* in due time Christ died for the *ungodly. . . . God commendeth His love toward us, in that, while we were yet sinners, CHRIST DIED FOR US. . . .* And not only so, but *we also JOY IN GOD through our Lord Jesus Christ,* by whom we have now received the atonement" (Rom. 5:6—11 in part).

Christian friend, how long has it been since you bowed on your knees and thanked God for being *a God of love and compassion,* loving you when *you* did not love *Him?* How long has it been since you thanked Him for sparing you until you heard His Word and received Jesus as your Saviour? If you have never prayed such a prayer of thanksgiving, *do it NOW* even before you finish reading this message!

"Blessed be the God and Father of our Lord Jesus Christ, who hath blessed us with all spiritual blessings in heavenly places in Christ: according as He hath chosen us in Him before the foundation of the world, that we should be holy and without blame before Him *in love*... to the praise of the glory of *His grace, wherein He hath made us accepted IN THE BELOVED*" (Eph. 1:3—6 in part).

Who but *God* would love hell-deserving sinners enough to set forth His Son to die in our place? Who but *God* would make us "accepted in the Beloved" and justify us freely from all things when we believe on His Son, thus making us holy, righteous, and free from guilt?

Listen to this: "You hath He quickened, who were dead in trespasses and sins: wherein in time past ye walked according to the course of this world, according to the prince of the power of the air, the spirit that now worketh in the children of disobedience: among whom also we all had our conversation in times past in the lusts of our flesh, fulfilling the desires of the flesh and of the mind; and were by nature the children of wrath, even as others. *BUT GOD, who is rich in mercy, for His great love wherewith He loved us, even when we were dead in sins, hath quickened us together with Christ,* (by grace ye are saved;) *and hath raised us up together, and made us sit together in heavenly places IN CHRIST JESUS, that in the ages to come HE MIGHT SHEW THE EXCEEDING RICHES OF HIS GRACE in His kindness toward us through Christ Jesus.* For by grace are ye saved through faith; and that not of yourselves: it is the gift of God: not of works, lest any man should boast. For we are His workmanship, created in Christ Jesus unto good works, which God hath before ordained that we should walk in them" (Eph. 2:1—10).

It is *God's great LOVE* that makes the difference in men. Those who have *accepted* God's love into their hearts are godly men who live godly lives. Those who have *rejected* the love of God are ungodly men who live *ungodly* lives. "Hereby perceive we the love of God, because *He laid down His life for us...*" (I John 3:16). Jesus died for *you!* Are you *living* for *Him?*

III
The Will of God Is the Bliss of Heaven's Glory

"Love not the world, neither the things that are in the world. If any man love the world, the love of the Father is not in him. For all that is in the world—the lust of the flesh, and the lust of the eyes, and the pride of life—is not of the Father, but is of the world. And the world passeth away, and the lust thereof: *but he that doeth the will of God abideth for ever*" (I John 2:15—17).

125

Here we are given a clear command: *"Love not the WORLD"*—and "the world" is clearly defined: the lust of *the flesh,* the lust of *the eyes,* the *pride of life.* One day the world and its works will be burned up—"the day of the Lord will come as a thief in the night; in the which the heavens shall pass away with a great noise, and the elements shall melt with fervent heat, the earth also and the works that are therein shall be burned up" (II Pet. 3:10). But John declares, *"He that doeth THE WILL OF GOD abideth forever!"*

What IS "the will of God"? The only place to find the right answer is in *the Word of God.* There is much in the New Testament on that subject. Jesus Himself had much to say about it. In His conversation with the woman of Samaria—a conversation which led to her conversion—He did not take time to eat the food His disciples had brought Him. They did not understand this, and they said to Him, *"Master, eat!"* He replied, "I have meat to eat that ye know not of. . . . *MY meat* is to do *the will of Him that sent me,* and to finish His work" (John 4:31—34).

If the one aim and desire of *the Son of God* was to do the *will* of God, then *what was* the will of God concerning the mission of Jesus on earth? According to God's Word, the only begotten Son of God came into the world for one purpose—*"to seek and to save that which was lost"* (Luke 19:10). Admittedly He did many other things while He

126

walked among men, but His one main reason for taking a body of humiliation and coming into the world was to save lost mankind. Matthew 20:28 tells us that "the Son of man came not to be ministered unto, *but to minister, and to give His life a ransom for many.*"

Everything else He did during His earthly ministry was secondary to His primary reason for coming into the world. He was on earth to do His Father's will, and the Father was "not willing that any should perish, but that all should come to repentance" (II Pet. 3:9).

In John 5:30 Jesus said, "I can *of mine own self* do nothing: as I hear, I judge: and my judgment is just, because *I seek not mine own will, but the will of the Father which hath sent me.*" In John 6:38–40 He made the same declaration—"I came down from heaven, not to do mine own will, but the will of Him that sent me"—and then added: *"THIS is the Father's will* which hath sent me, that of all which He hath given me I should lose nothing, but should raise it up again at the last day. And *this is the will of Him that sent me: that EVERY ONE which seeth the Son, and BELIEVETH ON HIM, MAY HAVE EVERLASTING LIFE:* and I will raise him up at the last day!"

So we see clearly that it is the will of God to save everyone who *"seeth the Son* and *believeth* on Him."* Of course this does not speak of *physical* sight, but the entrance of God's Word brings light, and through the Word, *with the eye of FAITH we see* that God loves us, Jesus died for us, and when we believe with the heart God saves us. We know that not all men are saved, and not all men will be saved in the future; but that is not because God does not *want* them to be saved. It is because they steadfastly refuse to believe in the finished work of Jesus for salvation.

In this wonderful day of God's grace we have much more light on spiritual values than the Old Testament saints had. We have "the perfect law of liberty" (James 1:25), "that which is perfect is come" (I Cor. 13:10). In other words, we have the Word of God in its entirety, therefore we have knowledge and understanding not afforded the Old Testament Christians. God has "made known unto us the mystery of His will, according to His good pleasure which He hath purposed in Himself" (Eph. 1:9). He has revealed that "we have obtained an inheritance, being predestinated according to the purpose of Him who worketh all things after the counsel of His own will" (Eph. 1:11). He has assured us that we are "sealed with that Holy Spirit of promise, which is the earnest of our inheritance until the redemption of the purchased possession" (Eph. 1:13, 14).

The New Testament Church is the Pearl of Great Price, and throughout the ages of ages God will show the exceeding riches of His grace when the Church is put on display in the Pearly White City, when all things are created new. The Church is made up of all born again believers, and the seal of the Holy Spirit is our assurance and guarantee that we will be present when the "purchased possession" is presented to Jesus—"a glorious Church, not having spot, or wrinkle, or any such thing . . . holy and without blemish" (Eph. 5:27).

Everything Jesus did while He was here on earth was done to the glory and honor of God the Father. Concerning the Old Testament sacrifices Paul declared, "It is not possible that the blood of *bulls and of goats* should take away sins." And then we read, "Wherefore when He (Jesus) cometh into the world, He saith, *Sacrifice and offering thou wouldest not, but a body hast thou prepared me: In burnt-offerings and sacrifices for sin thou hast had no pleasure. Then said I, Lo, I COME (in the volume of the book it is written of me,) TO DO THY WILL, O GOD.* Above when He said, *Sacrifice and offering and burnt-offerings and offering for sin thou wouldest not, neither hadst pleasure therein; which are offered by the law.* Then said He, *Lo, I COME TO DO THY WILL, O GOD.* He taketh away the first, that He may establish the second. *By the which WILL we are sanctified* through the offering of the body of Jesus Christ once for all" (Heb. 10:4—10).

Jesus came into this world to do the Father's will, and every moment of His earthly life was spent in *doing* the Father's will. Hear these words from His prayer recorded in John chapter 17—the prayer offered just before Calvary:

"I have glorified thee on the earth: I have finished the work which thou gavest me to do.... I have manifested thy name unto the men which thou gavest me out of the world:... Now they have known that all things whatsoever thou hast given me are of thee. For I have given unto them the words which thou gavest me . . . And all mine are thine . . . I have given them thy Word . . . And the glory which thou gavest me I have given them . . . I have declared unto them thy name" (John 17:4—26 in part).

With Jesus, it was always the Father's will, first and foremost—and we must never forget that God saves us for Jesus' sake (Eph. 4:32; I John 2:12). As believers, the way we can bring glory and honor to the name of Jesus is to be in the center of God's will, doing the will of God at all times. Paul says, "Whether therefore ye eat, or drink, or *whatsoever ye do,* do all to the glory of God" (I Cor. 10:31).

The will of God as related to the spiritual life of the believer is summarized in the following Scriptures:

"As many as received Him, to them gave He power to become the sons of God, even to them that believe on His name: *which were born*—not of blood, nor of the will of the flesh, nor of the will of man, *but (of the will) OF GOD*" (John 1:12, 13).

Then in James 1:18 we read, *"Of (God's) OWN WILL begat He us* with the Word of Truth, that we should be a kind of firstfruits of His creatures."

In I Thessalonians 4:3, Paul tells us, *"This is the WILL OF GOD, even your sanctification...."*

Again to the believers at Thessalonica, Paul wrote, "In every thing *give thanks,* for *this is THE WILL OF GOD...concerning you"* (I Thess. 5:18).

So you see, it is not only *the will of God* that we become *children* of God, it is also His will to fully equip His children to live a victorious, abundant, Christian life; and if we would be ever pleasing to Him we must live a life of thanksgiving. We *can* give thanks in everything because we have the assurance "that all things work together for good to them that love God, to them who are the called according to His purpose" (Rom. 8:28).

Salvation does not guarantee a bed of roses or a voyage without storms, but the Word of God offers this promise: *"If ye suffer for righteousness' sake, HAPPY ARE YE:* and be not afraid of their terror, neither be troubled...For it is better, *if the WILL OF GOD be so,* that ye suffer for well doing, than for evil doing" (I Pet. 3:14, 17). In other words, if we are living *in the will of God* and He calls on us to suffer, then *we glorify Him* in our suffering and we will be rewarded accordingly. However, if we are living *out of* the will of God and we suffer, we do not bring glory and honor to Him.

"Forasmuch then as Christ hath suffered for us

in the flesh, arm yourselves likewise *with the same mind:* for he that hath suffered in the flesh hath ceased from sin, that he no longer should live the rest of his time in the flesh to the lusts of men, but to *the will of God....* Wherefore *let them that suffer according to THE WILL OF GOD commit the keeping of their souls to Him* in well doing, as unto a faithful Creator" (I Pet. 4:1, 2, 19).

The believer who begins his Christian life in the will of God, continues in the will of God, and lives where he should live—in the center of God's will—need have no fear. Such a child of God may suffer and encounter hardship, but suffering for Christ's sake brings blessing to the Christian and brings glory to God.

IV

The Present Possessions and Privileges of the Children of God

"Behold, what manner of love the Father hath bestowed upon us, that we should be called the sons of God: therefore the world knoweth us not, because it knew HIM not. Beloved, now are we the sons of God, and it doth not yet appear what we shall be: but we know that, when He shall appear, we shall be like Him; for we shall see Him as He is. And every man that hath this hope in him purifieth himself, even as He is pure.... In this the children of God are manifest, and the children of the devil: whosoever doeth not righteousness is not

of God, neither he that loveth not his brother"
(I John 3:1—3, 10).

The new birth is the greatest miracle since the
virgin birth of Jesus! When a child of the devil is
born into the family of God, born from above, a
great and mighty miracle is wrought. You see, beloved, being *born again* is not simply changing
from a "bad" person to a "good" person. Determined *reformation* can accomplish that. When a
person is born again he becomes *a new creation:*
"If any man be in Christ, he is a new creature: old
things are passed away; behold, all things are
become new" (II Cor. 5:17).

When a person is born again he becomes *a possessor of divine nature:* "Whereby are given unto
us exceeding great and precious promises: that by
these ye might be partakers of the divine nature,
having escaped the corruption that is in the world
through lust" (II Pet. 1:4).

When a person is born again he becomes a member of the family of God, one of the *children of
God*—"and if children, then heirs; heirs of God,
and joint-heirs with Christ; if so be that we suffer
with Him, that we may be also glorified together"
(Rom. 8:17).

There are many Christians who do not enjoy
their spiritual birthright because they do not know
their standing in spiritual things. They are *beset
by fear* in the present life and *filled with doubt*
concerning the future. They fear losing their

salvation, they fear not being able to measure up to the standards of Christian living, they have no assurance of what the future holds for them in their relationship to God. Such fears and doubts hinder them from becoming effective soul-winners—which is what the devil delights in doing! If he cannot damn a soul, he sets about with everything in his power to rob that soul of its spiritual birthright and eternal reward—and in thousands of cases he does a very effective job!

Children of God NOW:—

John wrote, *"Beloved, NOW are we the sons of God!"* We do not wait until we reach heaven, this is not something that is in the future, something that will take place at some future date. *Believers are sons of God NOW,* this very moment, the moment Christ comes into the heart by faith. If we have salvation, we have been *born of God* and we are just as much a child of God the moment we are born from above as we are children of our earthly fathers the moment we come into this world. The new birth takes place when we hear and believe the Word of God, receive His Word by faith, take Jesus as our Saviour, and the engrafted Word saves our soul.

The Holy Spirit and Salvation:—

The Holy Spirit, the third Person of the Godhead, is the attending Physician at the spiritual birth: "Except a man be born... of the *Spirit,* he cannot enter into the kingdom of God" (John 3:5). The Holy Spirit convicts men of sin, draws them to God, opens the heart, and brings forth the new birth. Jesus made it very plain that no man can come to God unless he is *drawn* to God, and it is the Holy Spirit who does the "drawing." (Read John 6:44.) That is why it is so important that anyone who is convicted of sin not put off salvation. When God calls, when the Holy Spirit is working in the heart of the sinner, when that sinner is drawn to God, *then* is "the day of salvation," *then* is "the accepted time." Men are not saved when they "get ready." They are saved when the Holy Spirit draws them to God by working in the heart. The unbeliever is dead in sin, he is led about by the devil, and he must be arrested and caused to *think* of his condition before he will turn to God. The Holy Spirit is the only One capable of arresting the hearts of wicked men.

When a sinner *hears* the call of God, when he surrenders to the drawing of the Spirit, receives the Word and accepts Jesus by faith, the Holy Spirit then "borns" that individual into the family of God and takes up His abode in the heart of the new-born child of God—"and if any man *have not* the Spirit of Christ, *he is none of His!*" (Rom. 8:9).

Not only does the Holy Spirit take up His abode in our hearts when we are born again, He also leads us into paths of righteousness. "As many as are led by the Spirit of God, they are the sons of God" (Rom. 8:14).

It is the Holy Spirit who assures us that we are truly saved: "The Spirit Himself beareth witness with our spirit, that we are the children of God" (Rom. 8:16).

The Holy Spirit is our divine guarantee that we will enter heaven and receive our inheritance. He is "the earnest of our inheritance until the redemption of the purchased possession, unto the praise of His glory" (Eph. 1:14), and it is by the Holy Spirit that we are *"SEALED unto the day of redemption"* (Eph. 4:30).

Jesus died on the cross to save us from sin, to redeem the soul. He is coming again to take His own unto Himself, and when He comes the second time He will redeem our bodies and will give us a body like unto His own glorious resurrection body. John the Beloved assures us, *"... WE KNOW that, when He shall appear, we shall be like Him;* for we shall see Him as He is" (I John 3:2 b).

Are you saved? If you are, you have everything to look forward to. If you are *not* saved you have *nothing* to look forward to but everlasting punishment in the lake of fire. "The way of transgressors is hard" (Prov. 13:15 b). Yes, the way of the transgressor is hard in *this* life—but it will be much harder in the life that follows this one!

V
God's Son Is the Center of All Revelation

"We know that the Son of God is come, and

hath given us an understanding, that we may know Him that is true, and we are in Him that is true, even in His Son Jesus Christ. This is the true God, and eternal life" (I John 5:20).

Without *revelation* there would be no salvation, and *without the Son of God* there would be no revelation! We *know God* because of His *Son:* "No man hath seen God at any time. *The only begotten Son,* which is in the bosom of the Father, *He hath declared Him"* (John 1:18).

Christ was with the Father from all eternity. There was never a time in the eternity behind us when God was not—God the Father, God the Son, and God the Holy Spirit. *But JESUS had a beginning*—almost two thousand years ago when He was conceived of the Holy Spirit and born of the Virgin Mary, God in flesh (Luke 1:26—35; John 10: 30; 14:9; II Cor. 5:19).

Jesus was the Word in flesh (John 1:14), and He came into the world *to declare God to man.* He was the *manifestation of LIFE,* the *manifoldness of LOVE,* the *marvel of LIGHT:*

"As the Father hath life in Himself, so hath He given to the Son to have life in Himself" (John 5:26). Jesus was *the Word of Life.* He IS life.

"God is love" (I John 4:8). Jesus was God in flesh, therefore *Jesus is LOVE.*

"God is light, and in Him is no darkness at all" (I John 1:5). Jesus was God in flesh, therefore *Jesus is LIGHT.*

137

When Jesus spoke, His words were words of love, truth, and light, *words of revelation.* Early in His public ministry He uttered words which are probably the best loved and most often quoted words in the entire Bible: *"For God so loved the world, that He gave His only begotten Son, that whosoever believeth in Him should not perish, but have everlasting life"* (John 3:16). There is enough truth, love, and light in that verse of Scripture to save the whole world if the world would only *believe* it!

The Son of God — Salvation: —

"Whosoever shall confess that Jesus is the Son of God, God dwelleth in him, and he in God" (I John 4:15).

Again I call your attention to the fact that "whosoever" takes in everyone and excludes no one. Salvation is through the Son of God — yea, *salvation IS the Son of God in our hearts BY FAITH* (Rom. 8:1; Col. 1:27; II Cor. 5:17). In the Gospel of John — the "salvation Gospel" — the word *"believe"* is used more than one hundred times, in one form or another, in connection with eternal life. The only way to be saved is to believe on Jesus — not simply to believe *"about* Him." To believe on Jesus is to trust Him, have faith in Him; and faith in Jesus brings saving grace (Tit. 2:11).

The Son of God — Victory: —

"Who is he that overcometh the world, but he

138

that believeth that Jesus is the Son of God?"
(I John 5:5).

This question is answered in the verse that
precedes it: "This is the victory that overcometh
the world, *even our FAITH!*" Truly born again
believers overcome the world. They may not live
sinless lives, they may not be perfect; but *they
do overcome the world,* and "whosoever doeth
not righteousness is not of God" (I John 3:10). The
power of God that saves us also *keeps* us (I Pet.
1:5), and believers today can have the same assurance of victory described by the Apostle Paul in
his letter to the believers at Rome:

"Who shall separate us from the love of Christ?
Shall tribulation, or distress, or persecution, or
famine, or nakedness, or peril, or sword? As it is
written, For thy sake we are killed all the day
long; we are accounted as sheep for the slaughter.
Nay, *in ALL these things* we are *MORE THAN
CONQUERORS through Him that loved us.* For
I am persuaded, that neither death, nor life, nor
angels, nor principalities, nor powers, nor things
present, nor things to come, nor height, nor depth,
*nor ANY OTHER CREATURE, shall be able to
separate us from the love of God, which is in
Christ Jesus our Lord*" (Rom. 8:35—39).

The Son of God—Assurance:—

"He that believeth on the Son of God hath the
Witness in himself . . ." (I John 5:10).

139

The *"Witness"* here is the Holy Spirit. He bears witness with *our* spirit that we are the children of God (Rom. 8:16). Just as salvation and victory come through the Son of God, so it is with assurance. I John 4:13 tells us, "Hereby *know we* that we dwell in Him, and He in us, *BECAUSE He hath given us of His Spirit.*"

When the Holy Spirit abides in our hearts, we *know* He is there. That is one reason why it is impossible to be a child of God and not know it. True, there may be *times of doubt* because of ill health or prevailing circumstances, but doubt will soon give way to assurance for the truly born again believer. We may not "feel" like saints all of the time, but we are not saved by "feeling." We are saved by faith in the finished work of Jesus, faith in His shed blood, and John the Beloved comforts God's "little children" with these blessed words of assurance:

"These things have I written unto you that believe on the name of the Son of God, *that ye may KNOW that ye have eternal life,* and that ye may believe on the name of the Son of God" (I John 5:13).

The Son of God—Confidence:—

"This is the confidence that we have *in Him,* that, if we ask any thing according to His will, He heareth us" (I John 5:14).

There is no reason why fear, worry, or doubt

140

should trouble the heart of a believer. We *know* that we are born of God, we *know* we possess the power of God in the Person of the Holy Spirit, we *know* we have victory in Christ, we have overcome the world because greater is He that is in us than he that is in the world (I John 4:4). Fear, worry, and doubt are the children of unbelief, and *unbelief* is the ugliest sin a Christian can commit against a holy God!

The Son of God—Revelation:—

We have already discussed this part of our inheritance in Christ. Jesus came to declare—or reveal—God to man (John 1:18), and Himself made this fact very clear. He said, "I and my Father are *one*" (John 10:30). He said, "He that seeth *me* seeth *Him that sent me*" (John 12:45). To Philip He said, "He that hath seen *me* hath seen *the Father.* . . . I am in the Father, and the Father in me" (John 14:9,11).

God's great love for man and His boundless grace toward man are both revealed in the Son, the only begotten Son, whom God gave to die for us that we might have eternal life—the gift of God (Eph. 2:8). The only part man has in his salvation is to receive Jesus by faith. God the loving Father has done all there is to be done, all He *can* do, to keep us out of hell. He has revealed His love for us, He has given His only begotten Son to die for us, He has given us His

Word to reveal to us the way of salvation, and He has given the Holy Spirit to convict us, draw us to Him, and dwell in our hearts when we believe on Jesus. And *all of this is in HIS SON*, the living Word.

VI
"Born of God" — the Involution of All Life

"Whosoever is born of God doth not commit sin; for His seed remaineth in him: and he cannot sin, because he is born of God" (I John 3:9).

This statement from the Word of God has frightened many believers. They read it and then rush hurriedly on, wondering what it means. Some Bible teachers have tried to explain that it means "one born of God will not be continually sinning" —and while this is true, it is not the meaning of this wonderful verse.

You see, the *last* part of the verse explains the *first* part—that is, whosoever is *born of God* does not commit sin "for (or *because*) His Seed remaineth in him, and (therefore) *he CANNOT sin.*" Why? *"Because he is BORN OF GOD!"*

Now—*what part of man* is "born of God"? And what is *the "Seed"* that "remaineth in him"? When Jesus said to Nicodemus, "Except a man be *born again,* he cannot see the kingdom of God," Nicodemus asked, "How can a man be born when he is old? Can he enter the second time into his mother's womb, and be born?"

142

Nicodemus was thinking in terms of the flesh, not in terms of the spirit. Jesus replied, "Except a man be born of water (*the Word*—John 15:3; I Pet. 1:23) and of the Spirit, he cannot enter into the kingdom of God." Then He explained to Nicodemus, "That which is born *of the flesh is FLESH;* and that which is born *of the Spirit is SPIRIT*" (John 3:1—6). Therefore, we see that it is the *spirit* of man that is born of God. The *flesh* is not changed when one is born of God. *Physically,* man born of God still hungers for bread, meat, and other physical foods; but *man born of God DOES NOT hunger after ungodliness, unrighteousness, and wickedness!*

Flesh will be flesh until the first resurrection. It is the *inner man,* the spiritual man, that is born of God. Many babes in Christ become disheartened and discouraged when, after they have been saved for a few weeks or a few months, they lose their temper and say something a Christian should not say, or do something a Christian should not do. As long as we are in this body of flesh we will say things and do things for which we are sorry—but the very fact that we *are* sorry in our heart proves that we are *saved!* Only *one SINLESS Man* ever lived, and that Man was the spotless Son of God. All others have sinned, and even *believers* will make mistakes until they depart this life to be with Jesus—and "mistakes" are *sin,* in spite of the teaching of some people to the contrary.

But beloved, *that which is BORN OF GOD does NOT sin!* The spirit of a born again man is the *Holy Spirit* abiding within, the Spirit of God. In Ezekiel 36:26 God promises, *"A new heart* also will I give you, and *a new SPIRIT* will I put within you . . . ."* The body of flesh is the house in which the spirit lives. God does not give us a new body when we are saved—we will receive a new body in the first resurrection. But He does give us a new spirit. The "old man" is crucified and the "new man" (the Holy Spirit) takes over. "Therefore if any man be in Christ, he is a NEW CREATURE: old things are passed away; behold, ALL things are become NEW" (II Cor. 5:17).

Now what is the "Seed"—*His Seed*—that remaineth in the man who is born of God? The answer is found in the Word of God:

In Matthew 13:3—9 Jesus gave the parable of the sower. The seeds he sowed fell on different kinds of ground—"some fell upon *stony* places, where they had not much earth, and forthwith they sprung up, because they had no deepness of earth; and when the sun was up, they were scorched; *and because they had no root, they withered away.* And some fell *among thorns;* and the thorns sprung up, and choked them. But other fell into *good ground,* and *brought forth fruit*—some an hundredfold, some sixtyfold, some thirtyfold."

Then in verses 18—23 of that same chapter,

Jesus explained to His disciples that the SEED is the Word, and the "good ground" represents the man who *hears* the Word and *receives it into his heart.* "With the *heart* man believeth unto righteousness; and with the mouth confession is made unto salvation" (Rom. 10:10).

That which is *born of God* is holy, righteous, *divine* (II Pet. 1:4). That which is born of God *CANNOT commit sin* because "His Seed *remaineth in him* and he cannot sin." Jesus, the living Word, lives in the heart of every believer—"Christ in you, the hope of glory" (Col. 1:27). How wonderful to know that when we are saved we are not left to travel this pilgrim journey alone. Jesus promised, *"Lo, I am with you alway, even unto the end of the world!"* (Matt. 28:20 b).

Every born again believer can say with David:

"The Lord is my Shepherd; I shall not want. He maketh me to lie down in green pastures: He leadeth me beside the still waters. He restoreth my soul: *He leadeth me in the paths of righteousness for His name's sake.* Yea, though I walk through the valley of the shadow of death, I will fear no evil: for thou art with me; thy rod and thy staff they comfort me. Thou preparest a table before me in the presence of mine enemies: thou anointest my head with oil; my cup runneth over. *SURELY goodness and mercy shall follow me all the days of my life: AND I WILL DWELL IN THE HOUSE OF THE LORD FOR EVER"*

(Psalm 23).

VII
The Spirit of God

"Hereby know ye the Spirit of God: Every spirit that confesseth that Jesus Christ is come in the flesh is of God" (I John 4:2).

All other spirits are *antichrist.* There were spirits of Antichrist in John's day, and there are spirits of Antichrist today. John warns, "Beloved, believe not every spirit, but *try* the spirits whether they are of God: because many false prophets are gone out into the world" (I John 4:1).

In the following passage, John also warns those who *support* the spirit of Antichrist:

"For many deceivers are entered into the world, who confess not that Jesus Christ is come in the flesh. This is a deceiver and an antichrist. Look to yourselves, that we lose not those things which we have wrought, but that we receive a full reward.

"Whosoever transgresseth, and abideth not in the doctrine of Christ, hath not God. He that abideth in the doctrine of Christ, he hath both the Father and the Son. If there come any unto you, and bring not this doctrine, *receive him not into your house, neither bid him God speed: For he that biddeth him God speed is PARTAKER OF HIS EVIL DEEDS*" (II John 7—11).

There were many "deceivers" in the world in

John's day, men who denied that Jesus Christ had come in the flesh. These are called "antichrists" in our present passage of Scripture. However, this is different from the Man of Sin who will appear after the Rapture of the Church, as set forth in II Thessalonians 2:7—12 and Revelation chapter 13. The Man of Sin, *THE Antichrist*, will be the devil in flesh just as Jesus was God in flesh. He will announce that he is God, he will sit in the temple in Jerusalem to be accepted as God, and will deceive millions. But the *"spirit of antichrist"* of whom John speaks has been in this world since the days of the apostles, and will remain here as long as the devil is out of the pit.

Today these men, known as "liberals" and "modernists," fill many outstanding pulpits in America and around the world. They present Jesus as "a good man . . . a great teacher," *but they deny His deity.* Just as John described them, they deny that Jesus Christ is come in the flesh. They do not deny that He was a man, but they do deny that He was *the GOD-Man.* This is the spirit of Antichrist, and all who believe this false doctrine will spend eternity in hell.

In order to be saved, it is a divine imperative to believe in the virgin birth of Jesus. If He was *not* conceived of the Holy Ghost and born of the Virgin Mary as the Word of God declares, then He was all that the Jews claimed Him to be—an impostor, an illegitimate, a son of fornication! But

He WAS conceived of the Holy Ghost, He WAS born of the Virgin Mary, He was none of those terrible things the unbelieving world declared Him to be. He was the virgin-born Son of God, God in flesh (Luke 1:35; II Cor. 5:19).

It is the Spirit of God that "borns" us into God's family. The power of God comes upon us when we are saved and a divine miracle is wrought in our hearts through the mighty power of the Spirit of God. Paul wrote to the Ephesian believers of his prayers for them, "that the God of our Lord Jesus Christ, the Father of glory, may give unto you the spirit of wisdom and revelation in the knowledge of Him: the eyes of your understanding being enlightened; that ye may know what is the hope of His calling, and what the riches of the glory of His inheritance in the saints, and what is the exceeding greatness of His power to us-ward who believe, according to the working of His mighty power, which He wrought in Christ, when He raised Him from the dead, and set Him at His own right hand in the heavenly places, far above all principality, and power, and might, and dominion, and every name that is named, not only in this world, but also in that which is to come: and hath put all things under His feet, and gave Him to be the head over all things to the Church, which is His body, the fulness of Him that filleth all in all" (Eph. 1:17—23).

All born again believers are members of the body

of Christ. We are "members of His body, of His flesh, and of His bones" (Eph. 5:30). This is accomplished through "the operation of God" (Col. 2:12), by the mighty power of the Spirit of God: "For by one Spirit are we all baptized into one body, whether we be Jews or Gentiles, whether we be bond or free; and have been all made to drink into one Spirit" (I Cor. 12:13).

The Holy Spirit baptizes us into the body of Christ the very moment we trust Jesus for salvation through His finished work and His shed blood. We are *called* by the Spirit, *drawn* by the Spirit, *convicted* by the Spirit, *born* of the Spirit, *indwelt* by the Spirit, *led* by the Spirit, *empowered* by the Spirit, *filled* with the Spirit—and *SEALED by the Spirit until the day of redemption!* Man cannot be *saved* apart from the Spirit of God, he cannot live *the Christian life* apart from the Spirit of God. The man who is not led by the Spirit of God is not a son of God—he is a son of the devil (Rom. 8:9, 14).

But the Spirit of God does more than all of these things. Romans 8:11 declares, "If the Spirit of Him that raised up Jesus from the dead dwell in you, He that raised up Christ from the dead shall also *quicken your mortal bodies by HIS SPIRIT that dwelleth in you!*" Who raised up Christ from the dead? The SPIRIT OF GOD! and that same Spirit will quicken the mortal bodies of believers who sleep in Jesus, and will raise them from the grave when Christ returns for His bride, the New Testament Church. The Apostle Paul explains:

"If *in this life only* we have hope in Christ, *we are of all men most miserable!* But now is Christ risen from the dead, and become the firstfruits of them that slept. For since by man came death, by man came also the resurrection of the dead. For as in Adam all die, even so in Christ shall all be made alive. But *every man in his own order:* Christ the firstfruits, afterward they that are Christ's at His coming.

"Then cometh the end, when He shall have delivered up the kingdom to God, even the Father; when He shall have put down all rule and all authority and power. For He must reign, till He hath put all enemies under His feet. The last enemy that shall be destroyed is death" (I Cor. 15:19—26).

Because Jesus lives, we shall live also. Because He conquered death, hell, and the grave, *we are "more than conquerors through Him."* And the Spirit of God will quicken the righteous dead when Christ comes to call His own up to meet Him in the sky.

Thanks Be Unto God For Himself

"That which was *from the beginning*, which we have heard, which we have seen with our eyes, which we have looked upon, and our hands have handled, of the Word of life; for the life was manifested, and we have seen it, and bear witness, and shew unto you that eternal life, which was with the Father, and was manifested unto us" (I John 1:1,2).

"In the beginning was the Word, and the Word was *with God*, and the Word *was God*. The same was *in the beginning with God.* . . . and the Word was made flesh, and dwelt among us, and we beheld His glory, the glory as of the only begotten of the Father, full of grace and truth" (John 1:1,2,14).

"And Jesus, when He was baptized, went up straightway out of the water: and, lo, the heavens were opened unto Him, and...the Spirit of God descending like a dove, and lighting upon Him: *and lo a voice from heaven, saying, THIS IS MY BELOVED SON, in whom I am well pleased"* (Matt. 3:16,17).

"For in Him (Christ Jesus) dwelleth all the fulness of the Godhead bodily. And ye are COMPLETE IN HIM, which is the head of all principality and power" (Col. 2:9,10).

It was God the Father who loved us before the world was. It was God the Father who gave His only begotten Son to die for us, that we might claim His wonderful salvation—the gift of God. In this message we have discussed *seven things ABOUT our God*, all of those things found in John's first epistle to God's "little children," things which were written *that our JOY might be full:*

I. The Word of God is the basis of all authority —"Let God be true, but every man a liar" (Rom.

3:4).

II. The love of God is the secret of godly living —apart from the love of God there is no godliness.

III. The will of God is the bliss of heaven's glory—anything we do, say, or live that is not in the will of God brings dishonor to His name.

IV. The present possessions and privileges of the children of God—since we *are* children of God, it must follow that we are also *heirs* of God and joint-heirs with Christ.

V. The Son of God, the Lord Jesus Christ, is the center of all revelation, and apart from Him there could *be* no revelation.

VI. "Born of God"—the beginning and continuation of the spiritual life.

VII. The Spirit of God—the power of the new birth, the power for victory over the world and, in God's good time, victory over the grave. The Spirit that raised up Jesus from the dead will quicken our mortal bodies, praise His name!

Dear reader, if you are saved, a child of God, bow your head and thank Him for your salvation!

If you are *not* saved, won't you bow your head right now and ask Jesus to come into your heart and save you? He will save you—and you will know it! "For whosoever shall call upon the name of the Lord shall be saved" (Rom. 10:13), and "the Spirit Himself beareth witness with our spirit that we are the children of God" (Rom. 8:16).

SEVEN PAIRS OF THINGS

Seven Pairs of Things

"Finally, my brethren, rejoice in the Lord. To write the same things to you, to me indeed is not grievous, but for you it is safe. Beware of dogs, beware of evil workers, beware of the concision. For we are the circumcision, which worship God in the spirit and rejoice in Christ Jesus, and have no confidence in the flesh. Though I might also have confidence in the flesh. If any other man thinketh that he hath whereof he might trust in the flesh, I more: Circumcised the eighth day, of the stock of Israel, of the tribe of Benjamin, an Hebrew of the Hebrews; as touching the law, a Pharisee; concerning zeal, persecuting the Church; touching the righteousness which is in the law, blameless.

"But what things were gain to me, those I counted loss for Christ. Yea, doubtless, and I count all things but loss for the excellency of the knowledge of Christ Jesus my Lord: for whom I have suffered the loss of all things, and do count them but dung, that I may win Christ, and be found in Him, not having mine own righteousness, which is of the law, but that which is through the faith of Christ, the righteousness

155

which is of God by faith: that I may know Him, and the power of His resurrection, and the fellowship of His sufferings, being made conformable unto His death; if by any means I might attain unto the resurrection of the dead. Not as though I had already attained, either were already perfect: but I follow after, if that I may apprehend that for which also I am apprehended of Christ Jesus.

"Brethren, I count not myself to have apprehended: but this one thing I do, forgetting those things which are behind, and reaching forth unto those things which are before, I press toward the mark for the prize of the high calling of God in Christ Jesus" (Phil. 3:1—14).

The Bible draws many *contrasts*. For example, it presents the contrast between heaven and hell, life and death, right and wrong, truth and error, light and darkness, true ministers of the Gospel and false ministers—and many more. These contrasts are circumscribed by a very common word— *"THINGS"*—a word known and used by everyone.

In the passage just quoted from Philippians, Paul declared, "What *THINGS* were *gain* to me . . . I counted loss for Christ. . . . I count *all THINGS* but loss for the excellency of the knowledge of Christ Jesus my Lord. . . . I have *suffered the loss of all THINGS* . . . that I may win Christ. . . . Forgetting those *THINGS which are behind,* and reaching forth unto those *THINGS which are before,* I press toward the mark for the prize of the high calling of God in Christ Jesus."

As we proceed with our study we will find Biblical contrasts between "things *before*" and "things *behind*"; "things *spiritual*" and "things *carnal*"; "things *old*" and "things *new*"; "things *visible*" and "things *invisible*"; "things of the *flesh*" and "things of the *Spirit*"; "things of *God* and "things of *man*"; "things that can be *shaken*" and "things *unshakeable.*" And as we go deeper into the message we will discern how wide a *gulf* exists between the highest ideals which govern the word, work, and walk of mortal man, and the ideals which govern Almighty God.

The Word of God clearly teaches (and it is eminently true) that when one is born again he becomes a new creature in Christ. Old things pass away and all things become new (II Cor. 5:17). That which is born of the Spirit is spirit; therefore the regenerated life moves in a sphere which is completely foreign and unknown to the man of the world. The things the believer once loved, he now hates; and the things he once hated, he now loves. The unbeliever loves the world, the believer loves the things of heaven.

As high as the heavens are above the earth, so high are the concepts of the new life above the old. As sinners, we lived for self. As Christians, we now live for God. Once we were citizens of an earthly realm. Now we are citizens of heaven. Once we laid up treasures on earth. Now we are laying up treasures in heaven. Once we were at home in this world. Now we are pilgrims and strangers in a strange land, looking for that city whose Builder and Maker is God.

Jesus left the Father's bosom and took a body of flesh in order to declare God to man (John 1:18). In John 3:13 He said, "No man hath ascended up to heaven, but He that *came down* from heaven, even *the Son of man WHICH IS IN HEAVEN.*" Therefore, even while Jesus walked on earth among men, *He was IN HEAVEN with the Father.* Everything in the life of the Lord Jesus Christ on earth was in definite contrast to the lives of the people with whom He mingled.

This is clearly set forth in Hebrews 7:24—27: *"THIS MAN, because He continueth ever,* hath an *unchangeable* priesthood. Wherefore He is able also to save them to the uttermost that come unto God by Him, seeing *He ever liveth to make intercession for them.* For such an High Priest became us, who is *holy, harmless, undefiled, separate from sinners,* and made higher than the heavens; who needeth not daily, as those high priests, to offer up sacrifice, first for His own sins, and then for the people's: for this He did once, when He offered up Himself."

Men seek the *applause and praise* of men. Not so with Jesus. He asked His enemies, "How can ye believe, which receive honour one of another, and seek not the honour that cometh from God only?" (John 5:44). The Lord Jesus Christ never sought the praise or approval of men. He lived and spoke and worked to the glory of His heavenly Father, and the Father honoured Him in all that He did. Three times God spoke in an audible voice, acknowledging His beloved Son in whom He was well pleased (Matt. 3:17; 17:5; John 12:28−30).

While Jesus tabernacled among men, He sought not His own things, but the things of others. *Men followed Him for loaves and fishes,* while *He* sought only to please God and to bless others. Men sought riches, fame, and honor—while the Son of God had not where to lay His precious head! He even borrowed Peter's boat to use as a pulpit from which to preach. He was despised and rejected of men, a Man of sorrows and acquainted with grief.

There should always be this same contrast between the children of God and children of the wicked one (John 8:44). Born again believers are IN this world, but we are not OF the world (John 17:14−16). The entire life of a child of God—in its *aims, concepts, desires,* and *loves*—should stand out in bold contrast to the aims, concepts, desires, and loves of the sinner. When a *professing* Christian and a sinner love the same things, do the same things, go to the same places, and hold to the same ideals, *something is DRASTICALLY WRONG!* *Believers* are a peculiar people, *in* the world but not *of* it, minding not *earthly things.*

THINGS OLD — THINGS NEW

"Therefore if any man be in Christ, he is a NEW creature: OLD things are passed away; behold, ALL things are become NEW" (II Cor. 5:17).

The salvation of a sinner (the NEW BIRTH) is the greatest miracle since the virgin birth of the Lord Jesus Christ. When an unbeliever comes to Christ for salvation, a definite work of grace takes place in his heart and a miracle is truly wrought:

He immediately becomes a partaker of divine nature: "Whereby are given unto us exceeding great and precious promises: that by these ye might be *PARTAKERS OF THE DIVINE NATURE, having escaped the corruption that is in the world through lust*" (II Pet. 1:4).

He is born from above: "Jesus answered and said unto him, Verily, verily, I say unto thee, Except a man be *born again,* he cannot see the kingdom of God. Nicodemus saith unto Him, How can a man be born when he is old? Can he enter the second time into his mother's womb, and be born? Jesus answered, Verily, verily, I say unto thee, Except a man be born *of water and of the Spirit,* he cannot enter into the kingdom

160

of God. That which is born of the flesh is flesh; and *that which is born of the Spirit is spirit.* Marvel not that I said unto thee, *Ye must be born again"* (John 3:3—7).

The believer is the product of God's workmanship, created in Christ Jesus: *"For by GRACE are ye saved through FAITH;* and that not of yourselves: it is the gift of God: not of works, lest any man should boast. *For we are HIS WORKMANSHIP, created in Christ Jesus unto good works, which God hath before ordained that we should walk in them"* (Eph. 2:8—10).

The believer is not the "old man" made over or repaired; he is *a "NEW MAN,* which after God is created *in righteousness and true holiness"* (Eph. 4:24).

In Colossians 3:1—10 we read: "If ye then be risen with Christ, seek those things which are above, where Christ sitteth on the right hand of God. Set your affection on things above, not on things on the earth. *For ye are DEAD,* and your life is hid with Christ in God. . . . Lie not one to another, seeing that *ye have PUT OFF THE OLD MAN* with his deeds; and *have PUT ON THE NEW MAN,* which is renewed in knowledge *after the image of Him that created him."*

The NEW MAN is Christ formed *in the INNER man*—"Christ in you, the hope of glory" (Col. 1:27); and from the inspired pen of John the Beloved we have these words: "No man hath seen

God at any time. If we love one another, *God dwelleth in us, and HIS LOVE IS PERFECTED IN US*" (I John 4:12).

I repeat without apology: *the greatest miracle since the virgin birth of Jesus is the NEW birth.* A tremendous change comes into the life of the sinner saved by grace, a change readily seen by all who come in contact with a truly converted person. Christ in the life cannot be hidden. The way a believer walks, talks, smiles, and acts proclaims that there is a difference in the inner man. The unsaved man is "dead IN sin." When he becomes a Christian he is "dead TO sin."

Old Things Are Passed Away

"And YOU hath He quickened, who were dead in trespasses and sins: wherein in time past ye walked according to the course of this world, according to the prince of the power of the air, the spirit that now worketh in the children of disobedience: among whom also we all had our conversation in times past in the lust of our flesh, fulfilling the desires of the flesh and of the mind; and were by nature the children of wrath, even as others" (Eph. 2:1—3).

"We ourselves also were sometimes foolish, disobedient, deceived, serving divers lusts and pleasures, living in malice and envy, hateful, and hating one another" (Tit. 3:3).

Thus does the Apostle Paul present a picture

of the unregenerate man—pitiful indeed! *All* unsaved people are dead, *spiritually* speaking. "She that liveth in pleasure is dead while she liveth" (I Tim. 5:6). But when we become new creations in Christ, *death passes away* because Jesus tasted death for us:

"We see JESUS, who was made a little lower than the angels for the suffering of death, crowned with glory and honour; *that He by the grace of God should taste death for every man. . . .* Forasmuch then as the children are partakers of flesh and blood, He also Himself likewise took part of the same; *that through death He might destroy him that had the power of death,* that is, the devil; and deliver them who through fear of death were all their lifetime subject to bondage" (Heb. 2:9—15 in part).

Jesus conquered death, hell, and the grave. He now has the *keys* of death and hell. To John the Beloved He declared, "I am He that liveth, and was dead; and, behold, I am alive for evermore, Amen; *and have the KEYS of hell and of death*" (Rev. 1:18). Therefore *saved people* will never die! We will depart this life, yes, if Jesus tarries; but we will never know eternal death for we have passed from death into eternal life. Jesus promised, "He that heareth my Word, and believeth on Him that sent me, hath *everlasting life, and shall not come into condemnation; but is passed from death unto life*" (John 5:24).

For the saved person, *love for this world* is also passed away. The unbeliever walks "according to the course of this world," but the believer is led by the Spirit; therefore he has a new walk. God's Word emphatically declares that those who love this world do not know Jesus as their Saviour. In I John 2:15—17 we are commanded:

"Love not the world, neither the things that are *in* the world. If any man love the *world,* the love of the *Father* is not in him. For all that is in the world—the *lust of the flesh,* and the *lust of the eyes,* and the *pride of life*—is *not* of the Father, but is *of the world.* And the world passeth away, and the lust thereof: but he that doeth the will of God abideth for ever."

The unbeliever walks according to the leading of "the prince of the power of the air (the devil)," the spirit that operates in the lives of the "children of disobedience." But believers are sons of God and no longer walk in the path of disobedience. God has delivered His children from the power of Satan and has put the Holy Spirit within the heart of every believer to lead and guide into the pathway of righteousness. In Romans 8:9—16 we read, in part:

"Ye are not in the flesh, but in the Spirit, if so be that the Spirit of God dwell in you. Now if any man *have NOT* the Spirit of Christ, *he is none of His. . . .* For as many as are *LED by the Spirit of God,* they are the *sons* of God. . . .

The Spirit itself beareth witness with *our* spirit, that *we ARE the children of God.*"

Glorious truth! Believers are even now *seated "in heavenly places* in Christ Jesus" (Eph. 2:6). We are dead, and our lives are "hid with Christ *in God"* (Col. 3:3), and by the Holy Spirit we are *"sealed* unto the day of redemption" (Eph. 4:30).

When a person is saved, *"old conversation"* passes away. As sinners, we had our conversation "in the lusts of our flesh," but that which proceeds from the lips is first manufactured in the heart. According to the words of Jesus, "Those things which proceed out of the mouth come forth from the heart; and they defile the man. For out of the heart proceed evil thoughts, murders, adulteries, fornications, thefts, false witness, blasphemies: These are the things which defile a man . . ." (Matt. 15:18—20).

The believer has a *new* heart, and as a wicked heart produces wicked conversation, so *a clean heart* sends forth *clean and wholesome* conversation. "Filthy communication" has been put away (Col. 3:8) and the conversation of the Christian is in the name of Jesus and to His honor and glory.

As *sinners,* we were "without Christ . . . aliens from the commonwealth of Israel, and strangers from the covenants of promise, having no hope, and without God in the world" (Eph. 2:12). Note: *"We WERE"*—we *were* many things, all of them *evil.* But as *believers,* those things have passed away. We are now children of God—*"Beloved, NOW are we the sons of God"* (I John 3:2). We are not *going to be* sons of God, we are sons of God NOW, in this present life, from the very moment we believed. Now we have hope. We are under the new covenant. The old covenant has been taken away because Jesus fulfilled every jot and tittle of the law and the prophets (Matt. 5:17). And "the grace of God that bringeth salvation" *also teaches us* "that, denying ungodliness and worldly lusts, we should live soberly, righteously, and godly in this present world, *looking for that blessed hope, and the GLORIOUS APPEARING of the great God and our Saviour Jesus Christ;* who gave Himself for us, that He might redeem us from all iniquity, and purify unto Himself *a peculiar people,* zealous of good works" (Tit. 2:11—14).

All Things New

What are the new things we have experienced? First of all, we are *new creatures,* new creations in Christ (II Cor. 5:17).

We have a *new Spirit*—the Holy Spirit. He is with us and in us. He walks by our side, He lives in our hearts, He comforts, teaches, guides, endues us with power from on high, fills us, and seals us against the wiles of the devil (John 14:16—18; Rom. 8:9, 14; I John 2:20, 27).

We have *a new fellowship*—an abiding fellowship with the Father, Son, and Holy Spirit (I John 1:3).

We have *a new walk*—we walk no longer in darkness, but as children of light (Eph. 5:8).

We have *a new commandment:* Jesus said to His disciples, "A new commandment I give unto you, That ye love one another; as I have loved you, that ye also love one another" (John 13:34).

We have *a new work:* Jesus said, "Lift up your eyes, and look on the fields; for they are white already to harvest" (John 4:35). He also said, "Go ye into all the world, and preach the Gospel to every creature" (Mark 16:15).

We have *a new privilege:* As children of God we are also *heirs* of God and joint-heirs with Jesus Christ (Rom. 8:17). Therefore Jesus promised, "Whatsoever ye shall ask in my name, that will I do, that the Father may be glorified in the Son" (John 14:13).

We have *a new responsibility:* As great as the privilege, so is the responsibility of the Christian. Jesus said, "I have chosen you, and ordained you, *that ye should go and bring forth fruit . . .*" (John 15:16). We must bear fruit—and all born again believers *will* bear fruit to some degree. Jesus told His disciples, "He that abideth in me, and I in him, *the same bringeth forth much fruit: . . .* Herein is my Father glorified, that ye bear *much* fruit; so shall ye be my disciples"

(John 15:8).

THINGS BEHIND — THINGS BEFORE

"Brethren, I count not myself to have apprehended: but this one thing I do: forgetting those things which are BEHIND, and reaching forth unto those things which are BEFORE, I press toward the mark for the prize of the high calling of God in Christ Jesus" (Phil. 3:13, 14).

The Apostle Paul penned these words under inspiration of the Holy Spirit. As Saul of Tarsus, this man had much of which to boast. As he himself testified, "If any other man thinketh that he hath whereof he might trust in the flesh, I more: Circumcised the eighth day, of the stock of Israel, of the tribe of Benjamin, an Hebrew of the Hebrews; as touching the law, a Pharisee; concerning zeal, persecuting the Church; touching the righteousness which is in the law, blameless" (Phil. 3:4—6).

As the most ardent persecutor of the Church, Saul had praise of the Sanhedrin and the religious leaders of his day. He was determined to stamp out Christianity. Luke describes him as having "made havock of the Church, entering into every house, and haling men and women committed them to prison" (Acts 8:3). He was a born leader, as well as an educated man possessing many talents.

Then one day, just outside the Damascus gate,

168

Saul of Tarsus met Jesus—and became Paul the Apostle. His testimony then became, *"What things were GAIN to me, those I counted loss for Christ. . . . I count ALL THINGS but loss for the excellency of the knowledge of Christ Jesus my Lord!"* Those things that would be counted gain to him, from the standpoint of the flesh, he now put behind him and reckoned them as refuse fit only for the garbage dump. (Read Philippians 3:4—14.)

But note: In lieu of the things Paul cast *behind* him he placed other things—*abiding* things. On the Damascus road he asked, "Lord, what wilt thou have me to do?" and from that day forward I doubt that there has been another person so completely dedicated to God as was the Apostle Paul—yielded body, soul, and spirit to the glory of God. He prayed to know—not only the power of Christ's *resurrection,* but also that he might know *"the fellowship of His sufferings,* being made conformable unto His death" (Phil. 3:10).

Perhaps no other man ever had as much to boast about, religiously, as did Paul; but when he put his former life behind him he did not look back. He never once expressed regret concerning the things he left behind. He never gloried in his background. His one ambition was to live and work in such a way that at the end of his earthly sojourn he could stand approved before Christ.

This is evidenced by his testimony given in Philippians 1:21: *"For to me to live is Christ . . . ."*

Things so cherished and counted worthy by Saul of Tarsus were now *behind* Paul the believer. Once zealous as a Pharisee and chief persecutor of the Church, he was now just as zealous for *Christ.* Israel in the wilderness looked back and longed for the leeks, onions, and garlic of Egypt (Num. 11:5)—but not so with Paul. Lot's wife looked back to Sodom, yearning for the things she had left in that wicked city (Gen. 19:26). Not so with Paul. He placed no value on the things that lay behind him. He knew that in Christ he possessed all things, and with his entire being he now reached forward *to "the things BEFORE."*

To the Corinthians Paul wrote, "Let no man glory in men. For *ALL THINGS are your's . . .* and ye are Christ's, and Christ is God's" (I Cor. 3:21, 23).

To the Philippians he testified, "I can do *ALL THINGS through Christ* which strengtheneth me," and then he assured them, "My God shall supply ALL your need according to His riches in glory by Christ Jesus" (Phil. 4:13, 19).

To the Colossians he wrote, "Beware lest any man spoil you through philosophy and vain deceit, after the tradition of men, after the rudiments of the world, and not after Christ. For in Him dwelleth all the fulness of the Godhead bodily, *and ye are COMPLETE IN HIM*, which is the head of all principality and power" (Col. 2:8—10).

The Apostle Paul was so occupied with the things of the Spirit, heavenly things, that he had no time to think or fret about *earthly* things. He cast aside the things he had once counted dear—religious prestige, power, applause of men— and forgot them in pressing forward to things *before*. In his own words, "I press toward the mark for the prize of the high calling of God in Christ Jesus!"

In spirit, the Apostle Paul was closely allied with Moses. To me, Moses was the "Paul" of the Old Testament, and Paul was the "Moses" of the New Testament. Moses could have been king of Egypt if he had gone along with the royal family of Egypt—but he saw something the Pharaohs did not see: *"BY FAITH he forsook Egypt,* not fearing the wrath of the king: for he endured, *as seeing HIM WHO IS INVISIBLE"* (Heb. 11:27). Moses saw beyond this life. With the eye of faith he saw "the Invisible One," and the earthly vision of the throne of Egypt vanished! Like Moses, the Apostle Paul looked beyond this life and declared, "Eye hath not seen, nor ear heard, neither have entered into the heart of man, the things which God hath prepared for them that love Him. But God hath revealed them unto US by His Spirit: for the Spirit searcheth

171

all things, yea, the deep things of God" (I Cor. 2:9, 10).

Small wonder then that this prince of apostles should write to Timothy, his son in the ministry, *". . . I know WHOM I HAVE BELIEVED, and am persuaded that He is able to keep that which I have committed unto Him against that day!"* (II Tim. 1:12). There were no "things *behind*" for Paul; they were forgotten in his pressing forward to "things *before.*"

Beloved, we have the same God and the same Saviour Paul had—and all of us have left things *behind* which need to be forgotten in our eagerness to reach outward and upward toward *"things before"!* We are sinners saved by grace, it matters not the depths of sin *from which* we were saved. God's Word makes no distinction, there is no respect of persons with Him. He emphatically declares that *THE BLOOD OF JESUS CHRIST His Son cleanses from ALL sin* (I John 1:7).

God help us to follow Paul's example. Christians should never look backward, but forward—seeing "Him who is invisible," seeing the glory beyond this life, doing *all that we do* to the glory of God. Let our prayer be:

"Lord, lift me up and let me stand,
  By faith, on Heaven's tableland,
A higher plane than I have found;
  Lord, plant my feet on *higher ground!*"

172

THINGS OF THE FLESH —
THINGS OF THE SPIRIT

"There is therefore now no condemnation to them which are in Christ Jesus, who walk not after the flesh, but after the Spirit. For the law of the Spirit of life in Christ Jesus hath made me free from the law of sin and death. For what the law could not do, in that it was weak through the flesh, God sending His own Son in the likeness of sinful flesh, and for sin, condemned sin in the flesh: that the righteousness of the law might be fulfilled in us, who walk not after the flesh, but after the Spirit.

"For they that are after the flesh do mind the things of the flesh; but they that are after the Spirit the things of the Spirit. For to be carnally minded is death; but to be spiritually minded is life and peace. Because the carnal mind is enmity against God: for it is not subject to the law of God, neither indeed can be. So then they that are in the flesh cannot please God.

"But ye are not in the flesh, but in the Spirit, if so be that the Spirit of God dwell in you. Now if any man have not the Spirit of Christ, he is none of His. And if Christ be in you, the body is dead because of sin; but the Spirit is life because of righteousness. But if the Spirit of Him that raised up Jesus from the dead dwell in you, He that raised up Christ from the dead shall also quicken your mortal bodies by His Spirit that dwelleth in you.

"Therefore, brethren, we are debtors, not to the flesh, to live after the flesh. For if ye live after the flesh, ye shall die: but if ye through the Spirit do mortify the deeds of the body, ye shall live" (Rom. 8:1—13).

Things of the Flesh

The Word of God settles it: "They that are *in the flesh* cannot please God." God gave up flesh in the Garden of Eden. He said to Adam, *"Dust* thou art, and unto dust shalt thou *return"* (Gen. 3:19), but He was not speaking of the spirit or soul of Adam. He was speaking of the flesh; and if *God* did not attempt to repair flesh, *WE certainly should not!* Yet for six thousand years men have been trying to repair what God gave up. They substitute a social gospel for the blood-bought Gospel. They substitute good works for God's grace, and clean living for God's righteousness—but to no avail. Flesh is *flesh*—always has been, always will be. The only way to deal with flesh is to turn it over to God—and the way to do that is to *be born again:*

"As many as received Him, to them gave He power to become the sons of God, even to them that believe on His name: which were born, not of blood, nor of the will of the flesh, nor of the will of man, but of God" (John 1:12, 13).

Jesus said to Nicodemus, "Verily, verily, I say

174

unto thee, Except a man be *born again,* he cannot see the kingdom of God. . . . Except a man be born of water and *of the Spirit,* he cannot enter into the kingdom of God. . . . Marvel not that I said unto thee, *Ye MUST be born again"* (John 3:3—7 in part).

God's law is holy and powerful: "Wherefore the law is holy, and the commandment holy, and just, and good" (Rom. 7:12). But the powerful law of God did not—yea, *could* not—justify flesh. "Therefore by the deeds of the law there shall no flesh be justified in His sight: for by the law is the knowledge of sin" (Rom. 3:20).

However, the law was not rendered powerless through any fault of its own, but *through the weakness of the flesh:* "For what the law *could not do,* in that it was *weak through the flesh,* God sending His own Son in the likeness of sinful flesh, and for sin, condemned sin in the flesh" (Rom. 8:3). The flesh *hindered* God's law; but *Jesus* took a body of flesh and in that body He did what no other man ever did, or ever could do: *He fulfilled the law*—every jot and tittle—for Jesus never sinned! He was "in all points *tempted like as we are, yet WITHOUT sin"* (Heb. 4:15).

When a sinner trusts Jesus and is saved, it is not the *flesh* that is redeemed, but the *spirit.* "That which is born of the flesh is *flesh* . . . That which is born of the Spirit is *spirit"* (John 3:6).

175

No matter how hard a person may try, he cannot "born" his flesh into the kingdom of God. It is the spirit, *the inner man,* that is born from above. *Flesh is doomed:*

"Now this I say, brethren, that *flesh and blood* cannot inherit the kingdom of God; neither doth corruption inherit incorruption" (I Cor. 15:50).

The religious leaders of Jesus' day gloried in the flesh. When He said, "Ye shall know the truth, and the truth shall make you *free,*" they replied, "We be *Abraham's seed,* and were never in bondage to *any* man. How sayest thou, Ye shall be made free? . . . *Abraham* is our father. . . . We be not born of fornication; we have one Father, even God." Jesus said to them, *"Ye are* of *your father the DEVIL,* and the lusts of your father ye will do!"* (John 8:32—44 in part).

There are professing Christians today who glory in the flesh. They boast that they came from a long line of Baptists—or Methodists, or Holiness believers, or whatever their denomination may be. They declare that their family has been Christian for generations. But that does not help the individual one bit insofar as salvation is concerned. Each of us must be born again—or die in sin and spend eternity in the lake of fire that burns with brimstone!

Those of us who *have* been born again know that the flesh cannot be trusted. Paul expressed this in his letter to the believers at Philippi. He wrote, "We are the circumcision, which worship God in the Spirit, and rejoice in Christ Jesus, *and have NO CONFIDENCE IN THE FLESH"* (Phil. 3:3).

Even at best, flesh is extremely weak and untrustworthy. Paul reminded the Romans of this when he spoke of the "infirmity" of their flesh. In Romans 6:17—19 we read: "God be thanked, that ye were the servants of sin, but ye have obeyed from the heart that form of doctrine which was delivered you. Being then made free from sin, ye became the servants of righteousness. *I speak after the manner of men because of THE INFIRMITY OF YOUR FLESH:* for as ye have yielded your members servants to uncleanness and to iniquity unto iniquity; even so now yield your members servants to righteousness unto holiness."

Flesh stands for the old life, *the SELF life.* It is the nature we received from father Adam, the carnal, fleshly man. And when we are born again the *flesh* is not changed—i. e., it is still flesh, but *divine nature* abides in the believer and we overcome because God (in the Person of the Holy Spirit) abides in our bosom:

"Whereby are given unto us exceeding great and precious promises: that by these ye might be *partakers of the divine nature,* having escaped the corruption that is in the world through lust" (II Pet. 1:4).

"Ye are *of God,* little children, and have over-

177

come them: because *greater is He that is in YOU, than he that is in the WORLD"* (I John 4:4).

Hear Paul's confession in Romans 7:18—25: "I know that in me (that is, in my *flesh,*) dwelleth *no good thing!* For to will is present with me; but how to perform that which is good I find not. For the good that I would I do not: but the evil which I would not, that I do. Now if I do that I would not, it is no more I that do it, but sin that dwelleth in me.

"I find then a law, that, when I would do *good, evil* is present with me. For I delight in the law of God after *the inward man:* but I see *another law* in my members, warring against the law of my mind, and bringing me into captivity to *the law of sin which is in my members.*

"O wretched man that I am! who shall deliver me from the body of this death? I thank God through Jesus Christ our Lord. So then *with the MIND I myself serve the law of God; but with THE FLESH the law of sin!"*

Self—the natural man, the flesh—is that of which David wrote under inspiration of the Holy Spirit, "Behold, I was shapen in iniquity; and in sin did my mother conceive me" (Psalm 51:5). Even though we do not like to admit it, there is *nothing good* in flesh. The only *good* in us is *GOD in us* (Col. 1:27; 3:3).

However, God has not left us in ignorance concerning the flesh, for the works of the flesh

178

are clearly manifest. In Galatians 5:16—21 we read:

"This I say then, *Walk in the Spirit,* and ye shall not fulfil the lust of the flesh. For the flesh lusteth against the Spirit, and the Spirit against the flesh: and these are contrary the one to the other: so that ye cannot do the things that ye would. . . . Now *the works of the flesh are manifest, which are these:*

"Adultery, fornication, uncleanness, lasciviousness, idolatry, witchcraft, hatred, variance, emulations, wrath, strife, seditions, heresies, envyings, murders, drunkenness, revellings, and such like: of the which I tell you before, as I have also told you in time past, that *they which DO such things SHALL NOT inherit the kingdom of God!"*

The things named in this passage as works of the flesh all emanate *from* the flesh, they *adorn* the flesh. Since the flesh is not subject to God's holy law, neither indeed *can* be, all who live *after the flesh* fail to satisfy God (they who are in the flesh *cannot* please God), and therefore they will spend eternity in hell. There is no possibility of integrating the things of the flesh and the things of the Spirit. They have not one thing in common, and they are continually at war, one with the other.

All who walk after the flesh will be judged: "The Lord knoweth how to deliver the godly out of temptations, and to reserve the unjust unto the day of judgment to be punished: but chiefly them that walk after the flesh in the lust of uncleanness, and despise government. Presumptuous are they, selfwilled, they are not afraid to speak evil of dignities" (II Pet. 2:9, 10).

Apostate teachers glory in the flesh, but *they* do not possess the Holy Spirit. Peter describes them as "wells without water, clouds that are carried with a tempest; to whom the mist of darkness is reserved for ever. For when they speak great swelling words of vanity, *they allure through THE LUSTS OF THE FLESH*, through much wantonness, those that were clean escaped from them who live in error" (II Pet. 2:17, 18).

I repeat: The only way to deal with flesh is to be *born of the Spirit*—and then present ourselves as living sacrifices to God. Paul said to the believers at Rome, "I beseech you therefore, brethren, by the mercies of God, that ye present your bodies *a living sacrifice*, holy, acceptable unto God, *which is your REASONABLE service*" (Rom. 12:1). When we trust Jesus for salvation and present our bodies a living sacrifice to God, we have the assurance that we are "COMPLETE in Him, which is the head of all principality and power" (Col. 2:10). Nothing can be added to completeness. In Christ our every need is met, and we are more than conquerors through Him:

"What shall we then say to these things? *If*

God be FOR us, who can be AGAINST us? He that spared not His own Son, but delivered Him up for us all, how shall He not with Him also freely give us all things? Who shall lay anything to the charge of God's elect? It is God that justi-fieth. Who is he that condemneth? It is Christ that died, yea rather, that is risen again, who is even at the right hand of God, who also maketh intercession for us.

"Who shall separate us from the love of Christ? Shall tribulation, or distress, or persecution, or famine, or nakedness, or peril, or sword? As it is written, For thy sake we are killed all the day long; we are accounted as sheep for the slaughter. Nay, in all these things we are more than con-querors through Him that loved us. *For I am per-suaded, that neither death,* nor *life,* nor *angels,* nor *principalities,* nor *powers,* nor *things present,* nor *things to come,* nor *height,* nor *depth, NOR ANY OTHER CREATURE, shall be able to sep-arate us from the love of God, which is in Christ Jesus our Lord"* (Rom. 8:31—39).

"HAVING THEREFORE THESE PROMISES, dearly beloved, let us cleanse ourselves from all filthiness of the FLESH and spirit, perfecting holi-ness in the fear of God!" (II Cor. 7:1).

Things of the Spirit

"Verily, verily, I say unto thee, *Except a man be born of water AND OF THE SPIRIT, he cannot enter into the kingdom of God"* (John 3:5).

There is no such thing as salvation apart from the work of the Holy Spirit. I know there are thousands of preachers in this land who preach that a person can be saved and then receive the Holy Spirit at a later time; but such doctrine is foreign to the Word of God—*so DON'T BELIEVE IT!*

The *beginning* of salvation is hearing the Word of God (John 5:24). The Holy Spirit takes the Word, and through the power of the Gospel He draws us to God, and God saves us. This is set forth in the following Scriptures:

In Romans 1:16 the Apostle Paul declared, "I am not ashamed of the Gospel of Christ: for *it is the power of God UNTO SALVATION to every one that believeth;* to the Jew first, and also to the Greek."

In John 6:44 Jesus clearly said, *"NO man can come to me, except the Father which hath sent me DRAW HIM . . . ."*

In John 16:7—11 He said to His disciples, "I tell you the truth: It is expedient for you that I go away: for *if I go not away, the Comforter will not come unto you;* but if I depart, I will send Him unto you. And when He (the Holy Spirit) is come, *He will reprove the world of sin,* and of *righteousness,* and of *judgment:* of sin, because they believe not on me; of righteousness, because I go to my Father, and ye see me no more; of judg-

182

ment, because the prince of this world is judged."

The person who does not possess the Holy Spirit *is not saved.* In the words of Paul, "If any man *have NOT the Spirit of Christ,* he is none of His" (Rom. 8:9b).

The believer is *led* by the Holy Spirit, and through the *witness* of the Spirit he is given assurance of salvation, "for as many as are *led* by the Spirit of God, they are the *sons* of God. . . . The Spirit Himself *beareth witness with OUR spirit,* that we *are* the children of God" (Rom. 8:14, 16).

Not only are believers called, drawn, born, indwelt, led, and assured by the Holy Spirit—we are *SEALED by the Spirit* until the day of redemption (Eph. 4:30).

It is through the Spirit that believers *"mortify the deeds of the body"*—and live (Rom. 8:13), and God's Word promises that if we *"walk* in the Spirit" we will not *"fulfil the lust of the flesh"* (Gal. 5:16).

There is no middle ground with God. People are *saved*—or they are *lost.* They either *have* the Spirit—or they *do not* have the Spirit. How is it with *you,* dear reader? Put your experience to the test. "Give diligence to make your calling and election sure" (II Pet. 1:10).

The person who is truly born of the Spirit will automatically bear the *fruit* of the Spirit. Just as surely as a fruit tree bears fruit of its kind, so will the *Christian* bear the fruit of the Spirit—"love, joy, peace, longsuffering, gentleness, goodness, faith, meekness, temperance" (Gal. 5:22, 23).

THINGS OF MAN — THINGS OF GOD

"What man knoweth the things of a man, save the spirit of man which is in him? Even so the things of God knoweth no man, but the Spirit of God. Now we have received, not the spirit of the world, but the Spirit which is of God; that we might know the things that are freely given to us of God. Which things also we speak, not in the words which man's wisdom teacheth, but which the Holy Ghost teacheth; comparing spiritual things with spiritual. *But the NATURAL man receiveth NOT the things of the Spirit of God: for they are foolishness unto him: neither CAN he know them, because they are SPIRITUALLY DISCERNED*" (I Cor. 2:11–14).

The Things of Man

These are the things which man is *of himself,* everything contained in the genius and wisdom of man. Created in the image of God, man is the highest form of life, the highest intellect, on earth. The wisdom and knowledge of mankind today is staggering! There are mental giants on earth, *modern-day Nimrods* who are attempting to build a tower to heaven—and the only thing that will stop them is the second coming of the Lord Jesus Christ.

184

But hear what the Word of God has to say about the wisdom of man: "I will *destroy* the wisdom of the wise, and will bring to nothing the understanding of the prudent. Where *is* the wise? Where is the scribe? Where is the disputer of this world? *Hath not God made FOOLISH the wisdom of this world? . . .* Because *the foolishness of God is wiser than men;* and the *weakness of God is stronger than men. . . .* God hath chosen the foolish things of the world to confound the wise; and God hath chosen the weak things of the world to confound the things which are mighty; and base things of the world, and things which are despised, hath God chosen, yea, and things which are not, to bring to nought things that are: *THAT NO FLESH SHOULD GLORY IN HIS PRESENCE.*

"But of Him are ye *in Christ Jesus, who of God is made unto us wisdom, and righteousness, and sanctification, and redemption:* that, according as it is written, *He that glorieth, LET HIM GLORY IN THE LORD*" (I Cor. 1:19—31 in part).

The things of man are those things upon which men rely, things in which they trust. Generally speaking, these are things men can see and feel, things upon which they build—and then boast of the building. The things of man are things man has accomplished through his own wisdom and ability—but in the sight of God man's ability is reduced to nothing and man's wisdom is utter foolishness!

The Things of God

"My thoughts are not your thoughts, neither are your ways my ways, saith the Lord. For as the heavens are higher than the earth, so are my ways higher than your ways, and my thoughts than your thoughts" (Isa. 55:8, 9).

"O the depth of the riches both of the wisdom and knowledge of God! How unsearchable are His judgments, and His ways past finding out" (Rom. 11:33).

The things of God lie in a realm far above the human and the natural, and *no man* can know the things of God apart from the new birth. I Corinthians 2:10 tells us that God reveals things unto us *"by His Spirit,"* but the natural man, the unbeliever, does not have the Spirit of God, therefore he *"receiveth not* the things of the Spirit of God . . . neither *can* he know them, because they are *spiritually* discerned" (I Cor. 2:14).

Many men today are trying to put God in a test tube or on a slide under a microscope—but He cannot be found that way. God's Word asks, *"Canst thou by searching find out God?* Canst thou find out the Almighty unto perfection? It is as high as heaven; *what canst THOU do?* deeper than hell; *what canst THOU know?"* (Job 11:7, 8). No, God is not found by means of science applied in a laboratory. He is found BY FAITH—saving faith that comes from hearing the Word of God (Rom. 10:17). It matters not how much of this world's wisdom and learning man may have, *"without FAITH it is impossible to please God"* (Heb. 11:6).

But *through FAITH* we *can* please God—and *through faith* heaven is at our disposal! We see this in Matthew 15:21—28 when the Syrophenician woman came to Jesus and asked Him to heal her daughter who was "grievously vexed with a devil." At first Jesus answered her not a word. The disciples came to Him and begged Him to send her away. They said, "She crieth after us!" This was a Gentile woman, and Jesus explained that He had not been sent "but unto the lost sheep of the house of Israel."

"Then came she and worshipped Him, saying, Lord, help me! But He answered and said, It is not meet to take the children's bread, and cast it to dogs." The woman then said, "Truth Lord—yet the dogs eat of the *crumbs* which fall from their masters' table." Jesus then said to her, *"O woman, great is thy FAITH: be it unto thee EVEN AS THOU WILT!"* And her daughter was "made whole from that very hour." In other words, He said to this Syrophenician woman, "Be it unto thee *as thou wilt! Help yourself to anything heaven has!"* This dear lady wanted only that her precious girl be delivered from demons—AND SHE WAS.

Mark 9:14—29 records the account of Jesus' healing a young man who had been sorely tormented by an evil spirit. The boy's father said to Jesus,

"I spake to thy disciples that they should cast him out; and they could not." In the presence of Jesus, the boy—under mighty influence of the demon —"fell on the ground, and wallowed foaming." Jesus asked his father, "How long is it ago since this came unto him?" The father replied, "Of a child. And ofttimes it hath cast him into the fire, and into the waters, to destroy him: but if thou canst do any thing, have compassion on us, and help us."

Jesus then said to the man, *"If thou canst BELIEVE, ALL THINGS ARE POSSIBLE to him that believeth."* Read the entire passage in Mark chapter 9.

The most powerful force at our disposal is FAITH IN GOD, and the only way to have faith is to hear the Word. The more we study God's Word, the more we learn about God; and the more we learn about God the more FAITH we will have in Him.

The Gospels contain many statements like these:

"Believe ye that I am able to do this?" (Matt. 9:28).

"According to your *faith* be it unto you" (Matt. 9:29).

"Have faith in GOD" (Mark 11:22).

"He (Jesus) did not many mighty works there because of their *unbelief"*—their lack of faith. This was said of Nazareth, the home of Jesus, in Matthew 13:58.

188

God honors faith and blesses all who *exercise* faith. I Corinthians 1:21 tells us, "After that in the wisdom of God the world *by wisdom knew NOT God*, it pleased God by the foolishness of preaching to save them that *believe.*" (*Believing* and *having faith* are one and the same.)

Face it, beloved—it was the wisdom of this world that crucified Christ! The chief priests, scribes, elders—with all of their boasted scholarship, claiming to know the Word of God—crucified the Lord of glory.

The things of God can be known *only* by the *Spirit* of God. "For what man knoweth the things of a man, save the spirit of man which is in him? Even so *the things of God* knoweth no man, but the Spirit of God" (I Cor. 2:11). The Spirit "searcheth ALL things, yea, the DEEP things of God" (I Cor. 2:10). The Spirit is in the world to testify of Christ and to glorify His name. Therefore the Spirit will reveal to us all that we will receive and use to the glory of God. Jesus said to His disciples:

"I have yet many things to say unto you, *but ye cannot bear them now.* Howbeit when He, the Spirit of truth, is come, *He will guide you into ALL truth:* for He shall not speak of Himself; but whatsoever He shall hear, that shall He speak: and He will shew you things to come. He shall glorify me: for He shall receive of mine, and shall shew it unto you. All things that the Father hath are mine: therefore said I, that He shall take of mine, and shall shew it unto you" (John 16:12–15).

The spirit of the world does not know God. Therefore the spirit of the world *cannot reveal God to us.* Paul explained to the Corinthian believers, "Now we have received, *not* the spirit of the world, but *the Spirit which is of GOD;* that we might *know* the things that are *FREELY given to us of God"* (I Cor. 2:12).

May God help us to realize that the solemn Bible truths, *"the things of God,"* cannot be taught by man, by the spirit of man, nor by the wisdom of the world. *Be they ever so WISE,* men who are not born again cannot teach the things of God. Before man can teach the things of God he must first *be taught* of the Holy Spirit, and the Spirit does not dwell with the unbeliever. In God's love-letter to His "little children" we read: *"YE have an unction from the Holy One, and ye know ALL things. . . .* The anointing which ye have received of Him abideth in you, and *ye need not that any man teach you:* but as the same anointing teacheth you of all things, and is truth, and is no lie, and even as it hath taught you, ye shall abide in Him" (I John 2:20, 27).

No matter how humble a believer may be, no matter how untaught by the standards of men, he is a possessor of the Holy Spirit—the Author and Teacher of the Word of God; *and he can know ALL THINGS spiritual* through the teaching of

190

the Spirit. The sad fact is that in this day and hour most Christians are "at ease in Zion" and they do not hunger and thirst after righteousness and the deep things of God.

THINGS OF EARTH – THINGS ABOVE

"If ye then be risen with Christ, *seek those things which are ABOVE*, where Christ sitteth on the right hand of God. *Set your affection on things ABOVE*, not on things on the earth. For ye are dead, and your life is hid with Christ in God. When Christ, who is our life, shall appear, then shall ye also appear with Him in glory" (Col. 3:1—4).

There are people living *in* this world who are not *OF the world*. Jesus said to His disciples, "If ye were *of* the world, the world would love his own: but because *ye are NOT of the world, but I have chosen you OUT of the world,* therefore the world hateth you" (John 15:19).

There are two groups of men on earth today: WORLD-centered men, and HEAVEN-centered men—and of course when I say "men" I am referring to mankind, the entire human race. The Bible gives examples of men who are typical of these two groups. Let us look first at those whose lives were centered in the world and things material.

Things of Earth

In Luke 12:16—21 Jesus gave a parable, saying,

"The ground of a certain rich man brought forth plentifully: and he thought within himself, saying, What shall I do, because I have no room where to bestow my fruits? And he said, This will I do: I will pull down my barns, and build greater; and there will I bestow all my fruits and my goods. And I will say to my soul, Soul, thou hast much goods laid up for many years. Take thine ease, eat, drink, and be merry. *But GOD said unto him, THOU FOOL! This night thy soul shall be required of thee. Then whose shall those things be, which thou hast provided? SO IS HE THAT LAYETH UP TREASURE FOR HIMSELF, AND IS NOT RICH TOWARD GOD.*"

Then in Luke 16:19—24 Jesus said, "There was a certain rich man, which was clothed in purple and fine linen, and fared sumptuously every day: and there was a certain beggar named Lazarus, which was laid at his gate, full of sores, and desiring to be fed with the crumbs which fell from the rich man's table: moreover the dogs came and licked his sores. And it came to pass, that *the beggar died, and was carried by the angels into Abraham's bosom.* The rich man also died, and was buried; and *in HELL he lift up his eyes,* being in torments, and seeth Abraham afar off, and Lazarus in his bosom. And he cried and said, Father Abraham, have mercy on me, and *send Lazarus, that he may dip the tip of his finger in water, and cool my tongue: FOR I AM TOR-*

MENTED IN THIS FLAME!"

Many Bible scholars believe that the farmer in our first passage and the rich man in the passage just quoted are one and the same man. This could be true, I do not know about that; but whether they were the same man or two different men, they were definitely married to the things of earth and they had no time to prepare for heaven. Heart, mind, and body were dedicated to making money, acquiring more of this world's goods. Every day was a holiday for the rich man. His treasure was on earth, all around him, and he had no time for anyone but himself—no time for pity on the poor beggar who lay at his gate, no time for God or the *things* of God that would enrich his soul. He said, "Soul, thou hast much goods laid up for many years"—but *"much goods"* cannot satisfy the soul! He said, "Take thine ease! *Eat, drink,* and be *merry!"* That is the language of the world, and they who live in pleasure are dead even while they live (I Tim. 5:6). Jesus asked, "What is a man profited, if he shall *gain the whole world,* and *lose his own soul?* Or what shall a man give *in exchange* for his soul?" (Matt. 16:26).

Poor "rich man"! One moment he had everything money could buy, everything earth could give him—but a moment after he died he was *begging* for just one drop of water to cool his parching tongue! Think of it, beloved—one second, *a multimillionaire;* the next second, *a beggar in hell!* All the multiplied billions of dollars on earth cannot buy one drop of water in the eternal abode of the wicked, those who have no time for God in this life.

The book of Ecclesiastes tells of "the man under the sun" who is typical of the man of the world. He *tried* everything, he *had* everything—*but all was vanity,* and his world-weary conclusion was, "Fear God, and keep His commandments: for this is the whole duty of man. For God shall bring every work into judgment, with every secret thing, whether it be good, or whether it be evil" (Eccl. 12:13, 14).

Man is so created that it is utterly impossible for him to be satisfied and perfectly content unless he is in the right relationship with his Creator. Without God, there is an emptiness in man which things of the earth *cannot* satisfy. So he searches, continually, until he finds God; and when man finds God he finds peace—peace *with* God and the *peace OF God.* Jesus said to His disciples, *"PEACE I leave with you, MY peace I give unto you—not* as the *world* giveth, give I unto you. Let not your heart be troubled, neither let it be afraid"* (John 14:27).

In Matthew 6:19—21 the Word admonishes, *"Lay not up for yourselves treasures upon earth,* where moth and rust doth corrupt, and where thieves break through and steal: but *lay up for yourselves treasures in heaven,* where neither moth nor rust doth corrupt, and where thieves do not break through nor steal: *For WHERE YOUR TREASURE IS, there will your heart be also!"*

Things Above

"For I reckon that the sufferings of this present time *are not worthy to be compared* with the *glory* which shall be revealed in us" (Rom. 8:18).

"For to me to live is Christ, and to die is gain. But if I live in the flesh, this is the fruit of my labour: yet what I shall choose I wot not.   For I am in a strait betwixt two, having a desire to depart, and to be with Christ; which is far better: Nevertheless to abide in the flesh is more needful for you" (Phil. 1:21—24).

"Therefore we are always confident, knowing that, whilst we are at home in the body, we are absent from the Lord: (for we walk by faith, not by sight:)   we are confident, I say, and willing rather to be absent from the body, and to be present with the Lord" (II Cor. 5:6—8).

These passages were penned by the Apostle Paul, under inspiration of the Holy Spirit—and where could we find a better example of the heaven-centered man than this prince of apostles who wrote of the things of God in such exultation, confidence, and perfect contentment?   He counted all earthly things as worthless—and *IN this world* he had such a grip on heaven that he longed to depart this life and be with Christ—which would have been far better for *him*. But also in this life he had learned to be content *"in whatsoever state"* he found himself (Phil. 4:11). As long as God needed him on earth he was willing to stay, and he confidently declared, *"I can do ALL THINGS through Christ which strengtheneth me"* (Phil. 4:13).

Paul had no fear of death, and when the time came for him to face martyrdom for the sake of his testimony he confidently declared, "I am now ready to be offered, and the time of my departure is at hand. I have fought a good fight, I have finished my course, I have kept the faith: *Henceforth there is laid up for me A CROWN OF RIGHTEOUSNESS, which the Lord, the Righteous Judge,* shall give me at that day: and not to me only, but unto all them also that love His appearing" (II Tim. 4:6—8).

It was Paul who explained that believers are *already* seated with Jesus "in heavenly places" (Eph. 2:6). Therefore the only proper sphere for the Christian's abode is the heavenlies.

It was Paul who declared, "Our conversation *(citizenship)* is in heaven; from whence also we look for the Saviour, the Lord Jesus Christ" (Phil. 3:20). Our Saviour is seated at the right hand of God the Father (Heb. 1:3), we are "hid with Christ in God" (Col. 3:3), therefore *our hopes center in heaven.*

196

Even though believers are pilgrims and strangers on earth, even now God "hath blessed us with all spiritual blessings in heavenly places in Christ" (Eph. 1:3). The Greek here reads *"heavenlies,"* not "heavenly *places,"* and the meaning is that which is *heavenly* contrasted with that which is *earthly.*

"The heavenlies" also signifies the sphere of the believer's spiritual experience as he is identified with Christ. Now let us look at some of the *ways* in which the believer is identified with Christ:

First of all, *in NATURE:* "Whereby are given unto us exceeding great and precious promises: that by these ye might be *partakers of the divine nature,* having escaped the corruption that is in the world through lust" (II Pet. 1:4).

The believer is identified with Christ *in LIFE:* "For ye are dead, and *your LIFE is hid with Christ in God.* When Christ, who is *our LIFE,* shall appear, then shall ye also appear *with Him* in glory" (Col. 3:3, 4).

The believer is identified with Christ *by RELATIONSHIP* to Him: "Jesus saith unto (Mary Magdalene), Touch me not; for I am not yet ascended to my Father: but *go to MY BRETHREN,* and say unto them, I ascend unto *MY Father,* and *YOUR Father;* and to *MY God,* and *YOUR God"* (John 20:17). "For both *He that sanctifieth* and *they who are sanctified* are all *of ONE:* for which

cause *He is not ashamed to call them BRETH-
REN"* (Heb. 2:11).

The believer is identified with Christ *in SERV-
ICE:* "As thou hast *sent ME* into the world, even
so have I also *sent THEM* into the world" (John
17:18). "Go ye therefore, and *teach all nations,*
baptizing them in the name of the Father, and of
the Son, and of the Holy Ghost: *teaching them to
observe all things whatsoever I have commanded
you:* and, lo, I am with you alway, even unto
the end of the world" (Matt. 28:19, 20).

The believer is identified with Christ *in SUF-
FERING:* "Unto you it is given in the behalf of
Christ, not only to believe on Him, but also to
SUFFER for His sake . . . That I may know Him,
and the power of His resurrection, and the fellowship of His SUFFERINGS, being made conformable unto His death" (Phil. 1:29; 3:10). "I (Paul)
. . . now *rejoice in my sufferings* for you, and fill
up that which is behind of the afflictions of Christ
in my flesh for His body's sake, which is the
Church" (Col. 1:24).

The believer is identified with Christ *in IN-
HERITANCE:* "The Spirit Himself beareth witness with our spirit, that we are the children of
God: and if children, then heirs; *heirs of God,
and JOINT-HEIRS with CHRIST;* if so be that
we suffer with Him, that we may be also glorified
together" (Rom. 8:16, 17).

The believer is identified with Christ *in FU-*

TURE GLORY in the kingdom: "Blessed be the God and Father of our Lord Jesus Christ, which according to His abundant mercy hath begotten us again unto a lively hope by the resurrection of Jesus Christ from the dead, *to AN INHERITANCE INCORRUPTIBLE, and UNDEFILED, and THAT FADETH NOT AWAY, reserved in heaven for you"* (I Pet. 1:3, 4). "And they sung a new song, saying, Thou art worthy to take the book, and to open the seals thereof: for thou wast slain, and hast redeemed us to God by thy blood out of every kindred, and tongue, and people, and nation; *and hast made us unto our God KINGS and PRIESTS: and WE SHALL REIGN ON THE EARTH"* (Rev. 5:9, 10).

Believers are a "heavenly people," citizens of heaven, and like the saints of the Old Testament we confess that we are "strangers and pilgrims on the earth." (Read Hebrews 11:8—14.) Since we have been quickened with Christ, raised with Him to sit together with Him in heavenly places, we need not marvel that the Word of God admonishes us to set our affection on things above—that is, we are to *fall in love* with things above and not love the things of earth. God's Word warns, "If any man love the *world,* the *love of the Father is not IN him!"* (I John 2:15). Peter tells us that Christians, "as strangers and pilgrims," should "abstain from fleshly lusts, which war against the soul" (I Pet. 2:11). Things of earth will vanish away, but things above will abide forever.

Dear reader, on what is *your* affection fixed? You cannot serve two masters. Are you laying up treasure in heaven? Or are you striving to reach that place on earth where your friends will say of you, "He is *well fixed*. His home is paid for, he has money in the bank, he has enough of this world's goods to retire and live in ease"? Remember, beloved—no matter how much earthly wealth you may have, if you have not been born again through faith in the finished work of Jesus *you are NOT "well fixed."* On the contrary, *you are IN A FIX!* If you do not have a home in heaven, *you have NOTHING.* You are less than a pauper. But you can begin this moment to lay up treasure in heaven by giving your heart and life to Jesus, *now.*

THINGS THAT CAN BE SHAKEN — THINGS THAT CANNOT BE SHAKEN

"See that ye refuse not Him that speaketh. For if they escaped not who refused him that spake on earth, much more shall not *we* escape, if we turn away from Him that speaketh from heaven: *whose voice then SHOOK THE EARTH:* but now He hath promised, saying, Yet once more *I shake not the earth ONLY, but ALSO HEAVEN.* And this word, Yet once more, signifieth *the removing of those things that are SHAKEN,* as of things that are made, that *those things which CANNOT be shaken may remain.* Wherefore we receiving *a kingdom which CANNOT BE MOVED,* let us have grace, whereby we may serve God acceptably with reverence and godly fear: For our God is a consuming fire" (Heb. 12:25—29).

Things That Can Be Shaken

We see here that there are *things which CAN be shaken,* and *things which CANNOT be shaken.* Millions today hear the Word of God; but they pay no attention to it. Such a person is foolish beyond words. He is building on sand. Jesus declared:

"Whosoever heareth these sayings of mine, *and DOETH them,* I will liken him unto a wise man, which built his house upon a rock: and the rain descended, and the floods came, and the winds blew, and beat upon that house; and it fell not: for it was founded upon a rock.

"And every one that heareth these sayings of mine, *and doeth them NOT,* shall be likened unto a foolish man, which built his house upon the sand: And the rain descended, and the floods came, and the winds blew, and beat upon that house; and it *fell:* and great was the fall of it" (Matt. 7:24—27).

This earth has been under God's curse ever since Adam sinned in the Garden of Eden. Paul tells us that the "whole creation" groans and travails in pain—and it will continue to groan and travail until Jesus comes again! (Read Romans 8:18—23.) Then when Jesus comes, the former things will pass away and He will make all things new—including this earth and the first and second heavens. Peter describes it thus:

"The day of the Lord will come as a thief in the night; in the which *the heavens shall pass away with a great noise, and the elements shall melt with fervent heat, the earth also and the works that are therein shall be burned up.* Seeing then that all these things shall be dissolved, what manner of persons ought ye to be in all holy conversation and godliness, looking for and hasting unto the coming of the day of God, wherein the heavens being on fire shall be dissolved, and the elements shall melt with fervent heat? Nevertheless we, according to His promise, look for new heavens and a new earth, wherein dwelleth righteousness" (II Pet. 3:10—13).

Not only will the earth melt and the elements explode, but everything connected with this earth will pass away. *"The WORLD passeth away, and the LUSTS THEREOF"* (I John 2:17). God does not repair that which has been marred and scarred by sin. He does not repair the soul of man when a man is redeemed. This is plainly and emphatically set forth in Scripture:

God gives the saved man a new heart and a new spirit (Ezek. 36:26; II Cor. 5:17). These bodies of corruption will not be repaired. God will give us a new body in the resurrection (I Cor. 15:51—55; I John 3:1, 2). God will not repair the earth, nor

202

the heavens just above us where the clouds and stars are. He will make ALL THINGS new, so the old must give way and be removed.

When God sets up the Great White Throne before which the wicked will be judged, there will be *a great moving:* "I saw a Great White Throne, and Him that sat on it, from whose face the earth and the heaven fled away; and there was found no place for them. And I saw the dead, small and great, stand before God; and the books were opened: and another book was opened, which is the book of life: and the dead were judged out of those things which were written in the books, according to their works. And the sea gave up the dead which were in it; and death and hell delivered up the dead which were in them: and they were judged every man according to their works. And death and hell were cast into the lake of fire. This is the second death. And whosoever was not found written in the book of life was cast into the lake of fire" (Rev. 20:11–15).

Beloved, I ask you in all sincerity, How many people do you know who are really and truly preparing for a home in heaven? Most people today are working, saving, planning, and living as though they expected to spend all eternity right here on this earth! Even those who are saved spend literally hours in preparation for this life—and only minutes thinking of "that home over there." How utterly foolish for sensible men to build on a foun-

dation that is sure to crumble and fall! But that
is what the majority of men are doing today.

Things That Cannot Be Shaken

Our quoted text for this part of the message
speaks of "the removing of those things that are
shaken, as of things that are made, *that those
things which CANNOT BE SHAKEN may remain.*"
The things which cannot be shaken are the things
which GOD builds—"wherefore we receiving *a
KINGDOM which cannot be moved . . . ."*

In Daniel chapter 2, as that prophet interpreted
Nebuchadnezzar's dream, we see the complete history of the course of the kingdoms of men—their
rise and fall, their overthrow and disintegration,
and the end of "the times of the Gentiles," Gentile world power. These things have happened,
are happening today, and will continue to happen,
exactly as revealed to Daniel.

The final world empire will be the Kingdom of
Heaven on earth, when King Jesus sits on the
throne of David and reigns in righteousness. Kingdoms of men shall be moved. They will crumble
and decay. But Daniel saw a kingdom that will
not be shaken, it will not decay or pass away. *The
God of heaven shall "set up a kingdom WHICH
SHALL NEVER BE DESTROYED . . . and it shall
STAND FOR EVER"* (Dan. 2:44).

Thanks be unto God, in these uncertain days
there IS something SURE AND STEADFAST!

The Rock which Daniel saw cut out of the mountain without hands is the sure Foundation, and all who build on this Stone shall stand forever. But beloved, if that Stone falls on *you*, it will grind you to powder! (Read Matthew 21:44 and Luke 20:18.)

The Lord Jesus Christ is the "stumbling stone" to Israel (I Cor. 1:23), and *to all* who refuse to *believe* (I Pet. 2:8). He will be the "smiting stone" to the Gentile world powers in the end time as recorded in Daniel 2:31—35. If you are a born again Christian, dear reader, you are standing on the Rock that shall never be moved. If you are *not* born again, your life is *on the rocks* and you have built on sinking sand!

Salvation is through faith in the finished work of the Lord Jesus Christ. We are saved by receiving Jesus (John 1:12, 13). He then dwells in our hearts in the Person of the Holy Spirit and by the Spirit we are SEALED unto the day of redemption (Eph. 4:30). We are *in Christ*—and we can say with David: *"He only is my Rock and my salvation: He is my defence; I SHALL NOT BE MOVED!"* (Psalm 62:6).

Glorious truth! ". . . *neither death, nor life, nor angels, nor principalities, nor powers, nor things present, nor things to come, nor height, nor depth, nor any other creature, shall be able to SEPARATE US from the LOVE OF GOD, which is in Christ Jesus our Lord"* (Rom. 8:38, 39).

FORMER THINGS – ALL THINGS NEW

"I saw *a new heaven* and *a new earth:* for the first heaven and the first earth were passed away; and there was no more sea. And I John saw the holy city, *new Jerusalem,* coming down from God out of heaven, prepared as a bride adorned for her husband.

"And I heard a great voice out of heaven saying, Behold, the tabernacle of God is with men, and He will dwell with them, and they shall be His people, and God Himself shall be with them, and be their God. And God shall wipe away all tears from their eyes; and *there shall be no more death, neither sorrow, nor crying, neither shall there be any more pain: FOR THE FORMER THINGS ARE PASSED AWAY.*

"And He that sat upon the throne said, *Behold, I make ALL THINGS NEW.* And He said unto me, *Write: for these words are TRUE and FAITHFUL"* (Rev. 21:1–5).

Former Things

What are these "former things" that are "passed away"? Our Scripture passage names some of them—tears, pain, sorrow, crying, and death. Regardless of whether you are saint or sinner, you have shed tears—and death has visited your family at one time or another. Here, for the first time in the Word of God, we face the "passing" of these "former things."

For each believing soul, the cross of the Lamb of God holds in it all the blessed fruition of deliverance from pain, tears, suffering, sorrow, and crying; but even the *most spiritual believer* does not *yet* see full deliverance. Some people say that believers should not be sick or suffer pain. They declare that believers suffer only because of lack of faith. Such teachers are ignorant of God's Word. I realize that many Christians suffer because of sin in their lives—and no doubt some of them *do* suffer because of lack of faith; but Holy Scripture declares that it is possible to be sick to the glory of God.

When Mary and Martha sent word to Jesus that Lazarus was sick, He said, "This sickness is not unto death, *but for the glory of God, that the Son of God might be glorified thereby*" (John 11:4). In many instances we are closer to God when we are sick than at any other time; therefore God gets more glory from our sickness than from our health. This is not always true, but certainly it is true in many cases and with many Christians.

Consider *Job*. He was a godly man, there was none other like him, he was "a perfect and upright man," and he feared God. (Read Job 1:6—12.) Yet Job suffered in his body, in loss of his family and material possessions, and in so many ways that he has become the classic example of patience, endurance, and faithfulness—*and in it all, GOD was glorified!*

The Apostle Paul—wholly surrendered to God, thinking only of spreading the Gospel of the Lord Jesus Christ, living every minute of his Christian life to the glory of God—suffered in many ways. He knew disappointment, heartache, deprivation, persecution even by his own countrymen. He endured hardship and danger, and when he prayed for the "thorn in his flesh" to be removed God replied, *"My grace is sufficient for thee:* for my strength is made perfect in weakness." Therefore Paul declared, *"I take pleasure in infirmities, in reproaches, in necessities, in persecutions, in distresses for CHRIST'S sake: for when I am weak, then am I strong"* (II Cor. 12:7—10).

The fact that tears, sorrow, pain, sickness and death relate, to a greater or lesser extent, to all peoples of earth does not mean that Christ cannot, or does not, heal. *He can—and He DOES!* Neither does it mean that Christ is not filled with comfort and consolation. He comforts us in our sorrow, He knows every tear that falls from the eyes of His children; but the bitter cup of "former things" will be with us until our Lord calls us up to meet Him in the air and we step inside the New Jerusalem with "all things made new." Some of God's dearest saints spend their days in wheelchairs or on beds of affliction. Christians get sick and die—and their death is prefaced by sorrow, sighing, and pain.

These "former things" do not pass away when

we are born again. They will not pass away *until this present order passes away.* As long as Satan is out of the pit, as long as there is sin in the world, *these things must be.* But thank God, there is a day coming when Satan will be put into the lake of fire and sin will be no more. Then will be the time when former things are passed away.

All Things New

"I saw a new heaven and a new earth: for the first heaven and the first earth were passed away; and there was no more sea. And I John saw the holy city, new Jerusalem, coming down from God out of heaven, prepared as a bride adorned for her husband.

"And I heard a great voice out of heaven saying, Behold, the tabernacle of God is with men, and He will dwell with them, and they shall be His people, and God Himself shall be with them, and be their God. And God shall wipe away all tears from their eyes; and there shall be no more death, neither sorrow, nor crying, neither shall there be any more pain: for the former things are passed away.

"And He that sat upon the throne said, Behold, *I make ALL THINGS NEW.* And He said unto me, Write: for these words are true and faithful. And He said unto me, It is done. I am Alpha and Omega, the beginning and the end. I will give unto him that is athirst of the fountain of the water of life freely. He that overcometh shall inherit all things; and I will be his God, and he shall be my son. But the fearful, and unbelieving, and the abominable, and murderers, and whoremongers, and sorcerers, and idolaters, and all liars, shall have their part in the lake which burneth with fire and brimstone: which is the second death.

"And there came unto me one of the seven angels which had the seven vials full of the seven last plagues, and talked with me, saying, Come hither, I will shew thee the bride, the Lamb's wife. And he carried me away in the spirit to a great and high mountain, and shewed me that great city, the holy Jerusalem, descending out of heaven from God, having the glory of God: and her light was like unto a stone most precious, even like a jasper stone, clear as crystal; and had a wall great and high, and had twelve gates, and at the gates twelve angels, and names written thereon, which are the names of the twelve tribes of the children of Israel: On the east three gates; on the north three gates; on the south three gates; and on the west three gates.

"And the wall of the city had twelve foundations, and in them the names of the twelve apostles of the Lamb. And he that talked with me had a golden reed to measure the city, and the gates thereof, and the wall thereof. And the city lieth foursquare, and the length is as large as the breadth: and he measured the city with the reed, twelve thousand furlongs. The length and the breadth and the height of it are equal. And he measured the wall thereof, an hundred and forty and four cubits, according to the measure of a man, that is, of the angel.

"And the building of the wall of it was of jasper: and the city was pure gold, like unto clear glass. And the foundations of the wall of the city were garnished with all manner of precious stones. The first foundation was jasper; the second, sapphire; the third, a chalcedony; the fourth, an emerald; the fifth, sardonyx; the sixth, sardius; the seventh, chrysolyte; the eighth, beryl; the ninth, a topaz; the tenth, a chrysoprasus; the eleventh, a jacinth; the twelfth, an amethyst. And the twelve gates were twelve pearls; every several gate was of one pearl: and the street of the city was pure gold, as it were transparent glass.

"And I saw no temple therein: for the Lord God Almighty and the Lamb are the temple of it. And the city had no need of the sun, neither of the moon, to shine in it: for the glory of God did lighten it, and the Lamb is the light thereof. And the nations of them which are saved shall walk in the light of it: and the kings of the earth do bring their glory and honour into it. And the gates of it shall not be shut at all by day: for there shall be no night there. And they shall bring the glory and honour of the nations into it. And there shall in no wise enter into it any thing that defileth, neither whatsoever worketh abomination, or maketh a lie: but they which are written in the Lamb's book of life.

"And he shewed me a pure river of water of life, clear as crystal, proceeding out of the throne of God and of the Lamb. In the midst of the street of it, and on either side of the river, was there the tree of life, which bare twelve manner of fruits, and yielded her fruit every month: and the leaves of the tree were for the healing of the nations.

"And there shall be no more curse: but the throne of God and of the Lamb shall be in it; and His servants shall serve Him: and they shall see His face; and His name shall be in their foreheads. And there shall be no night there; and they need no candle, neither light of the sun; for the Lord God giveth them light: and they shall reign for ever and ever.

"And he said unto me, These sayings are faithful and true: and the Lord God of the holy prophets sent His angel to shew unto His servants the things which must shortly be done. Behold, I come quickly: blessed is he that keepeth the sayings of the prophecy of this book" (Rev. 21:1—22:7).

How wonderful! Beyond the grasp of human imagination! A new earth, the New Jerusalem with walls of precious stones, twelve gates—each gate one great, perfect pearl—and the street of *pure*

212

gold. Think of the vastness of that city—fifteen hundred miles "foursquare"—that is, fifteen hundred miles wide, fifteen hundred miles long, fifteen hundred miles high! There will be no need for artificial illumination, not even a need for the sun —for Jesus will be the LIGHT thereof!

Yes, *ALL things NEW,* no trace remaining of anything that has ever been, no reminder of sin. The LIGHT of the New Jerusalem will give light to all of God's new creation. The nations of earth will walk in the light of it. The leaves of the tree of life will be for the health of the nations, with no more sickness, pain, or death. No *unclean* thing will ever enter that city. Praise be to God, what wonderful times lie ahead *for the redeemed!* Blessed be God the Father of our Lord and Saviour, Jesus Christ!

Dear reader, are YOU prepared for that city? Heaven is a prepared place for a prepared people, and only prepared people will go there. *"Man that is born of a woman is of few days, and full of trouble. He cometh forth like a flower, and is cut down: he fleeth also as a shadow, and continueth not"* (Job 14:1, 2). This life is a time to prepare for a better life—and if we *fail* to prepare, better had we never been born!

Jesus came that we might have life, and have it more abundantly (John 10:10). He has gone to prepare a place for us (John 14:6), and *we must prepare* for that place if we expect to enter there.

213

There is only one way to prepare for heaven, and that is *God's way* as clearly laid down in His Word:

"As many as *received* Him (Jesus), to them gave He power to become the sons of God, even to them that believe on His name: which were born, not of blood, nor of the will of the flesh, nor of the will of man, but of God" (John 1:12, 13).

"There was a man of the Pharisees, named Nicodemus, a ruler of the Jews: the same came to Jesus by night, and said unto Him, Rabbi, we know that thou art a teacher come from God: for no man can do these miracles that thou doest, except God be with him.

"Jesus answered and said unto him, Verily, verily, I say unto thee, EXCEPT A MAN BE BORN AGAIN, HE CANNOT SEE THE KINGDOM OF GOD. Nicodemus saith unto Him, How can a man be born when he is old? Can he enter the second time into his mother's womb, and be born?

"Jesus answered, Verily, verily, I say unto thee, EXCEPT A MAN BE BORN OF WATER AND OF THE SPIRIT, HE CANNOT ENTER INTO THE KINGDOM OF GOD. That which is born of the flesh is flesh; and that which is born of the Spirit is spirit. Marvel not that I said unto thee, YE MUST BE BORN AGAIN. The wind bloweth where it listeth, and thou hearest the sound thereof, but canst not tell whence it cometh, and whither it goeth: so is every one that is born of the Spirit.

"Nicodemus answered and said unto Him, How can these things be? Jesus answered and said unto him, Art thou a master of Israel, and knowest not these things? Verily, verily, I say unto thee, We speak that we do know, and testify that we have seen; and ye receive not our witness. If I have told you earthly things, and ye believe not, how shall ye believe, if I tell you of heavenly things? And no man hath ascended up to heaven, but He that came down from heaven, even the Son of man which is in heaven. *And as Moses lifted up the serpent in the wilderness, even so MUST the Son of man be lifted up:* that whosoever believeth in Him should not perish, but have eternal life.

"FOR GOD SO LOVED THE WORLD, THAT HE GAVE HIS ONLY BEGOTTEN SON, THAT WHOSOEVER BELIEVETH IN HIM SHOULD NOT PERISH, BUT HAVE EVERLASTING LIFE. For God sent not His Son into the world to condemn the world; but that the world through Him might be saved.

"He that believeth on Him is NOT CONDEMNED: but he that believeth NOT is condemned ALREADY, because he hath not believed in the name of the only begotten Son of God" (John 3:1—18).

"Verily, verily, I say unto you, He that HEARETH MY WORD, and believeth on Him that sent me, HATH everlasting life, and shall not come into condemnation; but IS PASSED FROM DEATH UNTO LIFE" (John 5:24).

"Believe on the Lord Jesus Christ, AND THOU SHALT BE SAVED, and thy house" (Acts 16:31).

"If thou shalt confess with thy mouth the Lord Jesus, and shalt believe in thine heart that God hath raised Him from the dead, THOU SHALT BE SAVED. For with the heart man believeth unto righteousness; and with the mouth confession is made unto salvation" (Rom. 10:9, 10).

"For by grace are ye saved through faith; and that not of yourselves: it is the gift of God: not of works, lest any man should boast" (Eph. 2:8, 9).

"If we confess our sins, He is faithful and just to forgive us our sins, and to cleanse us from all unrighteousness" (I John 1:9).

I ask you once more, beloved, Are YOU saved? Ask *yourself* that eternal question—and then answer it honestly. If you are not saved, do what these passages tell you to do—and Jesus will save you this moment. Just bow your head, and in your own words tell Him that you want Him to forgive your sins, save you, and prepare you for heaven—*and He will!* Now thank Him for saving you. Then write to me and give me your testimony so that I can rejoice with you.

SEVEN SETS OF BIBLE TWINS

Seven Sets of Bible Twins

"Enter ye in at the strait gate: for wide is the gate, and broad is the way, that leadeth to destruction, and many there be which go in thereat: Because strait is the gate, and narrow is the way, which leadeth unto life, and few there be that find it.

"Beware of false prophets, which come to you in sheep's clothing, but inwardly they are ravening wolves. Ye shall know them by their fruits. Do men gather grapes of thorns, or figs of thistles? Even so every good tree bringeth forth good fruit; but a corrupt tree bringeth forth evil fruit. A good tree cannot bring forth evil fruit, neither can a corrupt tree bring forth good fruit. Every tree that bringeth not forth good fruit is hewn down, and cast into the fire. Wherefore by their fruits ye shall know them. . . .

"Therefore whosoever heareth these sayings of mine, and doeth them, I will liken him unto a wise man, which built his house upon a rock: and the rain descended, and the floods came, and the winds blew, and beat upon that house; and it fell not: for it was founded upon a rock. And every one that heareth these sayings of mine, and doeth them not, shall be likened unto a foolish man, which built his house upon the sand: and the rain descended, and the floods came, and the winds blew, and beat upon that house; and it fell: and great was the fall of it.

"And it came to pass, when Jesus had ended these sayings, the people were astonished at His doctrine: for He taught them as one having authority, and not as the scribes" (Matt. 7:13—29 in part).

There is something fascinating about twins. Whether they be babies, teenagers, or adults, twins always catch the eye. Therefore as I read Matthew chapter seven I cannot help seeing *seven sets* of very *unusual* twins—unusual in that they are not identical, but *opposite,* as opposite as can be. There is a great spiritual lesson here. May God grant that we learn from these Scriptures that which He would have us learn.

TWIN GATES

"Enter ye in at the strait gate: for wide is the gate, and broad is the way, that leadeth to *destruction,* and many there be which go in thereat: because strait is the gate, and narrow is the way, which leadeth unto *life,* and few there be that find it" (Matt. 7:13, 14).

What IS a "gate"? Most of us think we know the answer to that question—but do we *really* know what a gate is, and what it does? Webster defines a gate as "an opening for passage in an enclosing wall, fence, or barrier, especially an opening with a movable frame or door for closing it. Also the frame or door which closes a gate; *any means of ENTRANCE or EXIT.*"

In the passage just quoted from Matthew we find *two* gates—one straight and narrow, one broad and inviting. The straight and narrow gate offers entrance to LIFE—or heaven. The broad gate is the entrance to HELL—or destruction. Since the only way to rightly divide the Word of God is to compare Scripture with Scripture, spiritual things with spiritual, let us look into the Word and see just what Jesus is really saying to us here.

Jesus is the gate (the door) to heaven. The dictionary definition of "DOOR" is almost identical with the definition I have just given for "gate." A door is "a movable object for closing a doorway." A door keeps the heat in and keeps the cold out. A door allows the family to enter the home but keeps out those who have no business in the house—robbers, thieves, anyone who would hurt or destroy. The Scripture tells us that Jesus is THE DOOR—*the only door*—to heaven. Thus He will permit *His children* to enter heaven and— believe it or not—He will see to it that *no one* enters there who is not saved! *He will also see that no one enters EXCEPT BY THE DOOR:*

"Verily, verily, I say unto you, He that entereth not *by the DOOR* into the sheepfold, but climbeth up some other way, *the same is a thief and a robber.* But he that entereth in by the door is the Shepherd of the sheep. To Him the porter openeth; and the sheep hear His voice: and He calleth His own sheep by name, and leadeth them out. And when He putteth forth His own sheep, He goeth before them, and the sheep follow Him: for they know His voice. And a stranger will they not follow, but will flee from him: for they know not the voice of strangers. . . . *Verily, verily, I say unto you, I AM THE DOOR OF THE SHEEP.* All that ever came before me are thieves and robbers: but the sheep did not hear them. *I AM THE DOOR: by me if any man enter in, he shall be saved,* and shall go in and out, and find pasture" (John 10:1—9).

They are thieves and robbers who attempt to enter heaven any way except by the DOOR— *through the finished work of Jesus;* and sad words are these: *"FEW THERE BE THAT FIND IT!"* There are multiplied millions who are *religious*— but "religion" is not a guarantee to heaven! Never has there been a more religious group of people on this earth than were the Pharisees and Sadducees who lived in the days when Jesus tabernacled among men; but in spite of their "religion" they were LOST. Jesus called them fools, thieves, robbers, "whited sepulchres" full of dead mens' bones, children of the devil (Matt. 23:13–33; John 8:44), *but not once did He call them His children.*

The masses have always gone the way of least resistance—the way to heaven is *too narrow* for them; but man was created with a desire to worship, and even through the fall he did not lose that desire. Therefore all men have "gods." *All* men are "religious"—but not all men are *saved.* The majority of mankind is lost and definitely on the road to hell.

Yes, *the BROAD gate* opens into hell, and the broad road is well traveled. But in spite of the fact that the masses are traveling the broad road and entering in at the broad GATE, we have the assurance that while Christians are in the minority, JESUS and the Christian make a MAJORITY! Believers are few, percentage-wise; but we are a majority victory-wise—and that is what counts. Jesus assured His disciples that *"the gates of HELL" should not prevail against HIS CHURCH* (Matt. 16:13–18).

Dear reader, you are headed toward the *NARROW gate* which opens into heaven, or you are headed toward the *WIDE gate* that opens into hell. *There IS no "middle" gate,* there is no *neutrality,* where Jesus is concerned. There are only TWO gates. Which one will YOU enter at the end of life's journey? If you are traveling toward *the broad gate of destruction,* God grant that you turn face-about and start toward heaven today!   You *can* be saved if you *want* to be.

TWIN WAYS

"... *Broad is the WAY* that leadeth to destruction, and many there be which go in thereat; ... *NARROW is the way* which leadeth unto life, and few there be that find it" (Matt. 7:13, 14).

The dictionary defines *"way"* as "that along which one passes or progresses to reach some place; a road, street, tract, or path." You will notice that the TWIN WAYS in our Scripture are not identical, but opposite. The *narrow* way (God's way) leads to LIFE. The *broad* way (the devil's way) leads to DESTRUCTION. As for *me,* I want to know the truth about the way that leads to life, so that I can tell men how to *find* that way. By like token I want to know the truth about the way that leads to destruction, so that I can *warn* men not to travel that way!

The Broad Way

Solomon said, "There is a way that seemeth right unto a man, but the end thereof are the WAYS OF DEATH" (Prov. 16:25). That is the tragedy of this hour—so many ways are presented by "religions," preachers, teachers. In desperation the poor sinner asks, "Which way is *right?*" I answer in the words of the Apostle Paul: *"LET GOD BE TRUE, but every man a LIAR"* (Rom. 3:4).

224

The verse from Proverbs first mentions "a WAY" (singular). Then it mentions "WAYS" (plural). Man has his "ways," but all of man's ways lead to the same destination—*hell!* A book of many pages could be written on "The WAYS of Man," religiously speaking, but we will look at only a few of those ways:

The Way of Religion:—

Some dear people think it makes no difference *what kind* of religion they have, as long as they faithfully attend church, take part in the church rituals and give of their money. I do not hesitate to declare dogmatically that *hell is filled with religious folks!* Almost *all* people have some form of religion, but when referring to salvation from sin the word "religion" is used very few times in our Bible. James 1:27 speaks of *"PURE religion"*—and then defines it; but James is speaking of *Christianity* in its true sense.

In most instances where the Bible speaks of "religion" it is referring to false religions and not to Christianity. For instance, when Paul testified before King Agrippa he said, "After the most straitest sect of *our religion* I lived a Pharisee" (Acts 26:5 b). It is true that Paul lived a *strictly "religious"* life. I doubt that there was ever a more dedicated religionist than Saul of Tarsus—yet he consented to the horrible death of Stephen, he "made havoc of the Church, entering into every house, and haling men and women committed them to prison" (Acts 8:1—3). Then he met Jesus on the Damascus road, he became a Christian, and he ceased to practice his "religion." (Please study all of Acts chapter 9.)

The men who demanded the death of the Son of God were "religious" men. Godless Pilate wanted to release Jesus and let Him go. Three times he said to the Jews, *"I find NO FAULT in Him!"* But the chief religionists of Israel demanded, "Let Him be *crucified!* His blood be on us, and on our children!" (Matt. 27:22—25).

Jesus offered salvation and liberty to these religionists, but they rejected His offer. Listen to this conversation between the sinless Son of God and the religious leaders of His day:

"Ye shall know the TRUTH, and the truth shall make you FREE. *They answered Him,* We be Abraham's seed, and were never in bondage to any man: how sayest thou, Ye shall be made free?

"Jesus answered them, Verily, verily, I say unto you, Whosoever committeth sin is the *servant* of sin. And the servant abideth not in the house for ever: but the Son abideth ever. If the SON therefore shall make you free, ye shall be FREE INDEED. I know that ye are Abraham's seed; but ye seek to kill me, because my Word hath no place in you. I speak that which I have seen with my Father: and ye do that which ye have

226

seen with your father.

"They answered and said unto Him, *Abraham is our father.* Jesus saith unto them, If ye were Abraham's children, ye would do the works of Abraham. But now ye seek to kill me, a Man that hath told you the truth, which I have heard of God: this did not Abraham. Ye do the deeds of your father. *THEN SAID THEY TO HIM,* We be not born of fornication; we have one Father, even God.

"Jesus said unto them: If God were your Father, ye would love me: for I proceeded forth and came from God; neither came I of myself, but He sent me. Why do ye not understand my speech? even because ye cannot hear my Word. YE ARE OF YOUR FATHER THE DEVIL, and the lusts of your father ye will do. He was a murderer from the beginning, and abode not in the truth, because there is no truth in him. When he speaketh a lie, he speaketh of his own: for he is a liar, and the father of it. And because I tell you the truth, ye believe me not. WHICH OF YOU CONVINCETH ME OF SIN? And if I say the truth, why do ye not believe me? He that is of God heareth God's words: Ye therefore hear them not, because YE ARE NOT OF GOD.

"*Then answered the Jews,* and said unto Him, Say we not well that thou art a Samaritan, and hast a devil?

227

"Jesus answered, *I have NOT a devil;* but I honour my Father, and ye do dishonour me. And I seek not mine own glory: there is one that seeketh and judgeth. Verily, verily, I say unto you, If a man keep my saying, he shall never see death.

"Then said the Jews unto Him, *Now we KNOW that thou hast a devil!* Abraham is dead, and the prophets; and thou sayest, If a man keep my saying, he shall never taste of death. Art thou greater than our father Abraham, which is dead? and *the prophets are dead.* Whom makest thou thyself?

"Jesus answered, If I honour myself, my honour is nothing: it is my Father that honoureth me; of whom ye say, that He is your God. Yet ye have not known Him; but I know Him: and if I should say, I know Him not, *I shall be a liar LIKE UNTO YOU:* but I know Him, and keep His saying. Your father Abraham rejoiced to see my day: and he saw it, and was glad.

"Then said the Jews unto Him, *Thou art not yet fifty years old, and hast thou seen Abraham?* Jesus said unto them, Verily, verily, I say unto you, *Before Abraham was, I AM!*

"Then took they up stones to cast at Him: but Jesus hid Himself, and went out of the temple, going through the midst of them, and so passed by" (John 8:32—59).

"Religion" is being *zealous*—"but not according

228

to knowledge." (Read Romans chapter 10.)

Christianity is knowing Christ by FAITH— "CHRIST IN YOU, the hope of glory" (Col. 1:27).

Now I ask YOU, dear reader: *Are you "RE-LIGIOUS"?* or *are you SAVED?* Religion never has saved a soul, and never will! The devil is determined to damn every soul he possibly can and he had just as soon see you go to hell from a church roll as from skid row! In The Gospel Hour files are thousands of testimonies from church members—*religionists* who have been saved by listening to our radio broadcasts or by reading a message such as this. Churches today are filled with people who are "religious"—but LOST. Only a small percentage of church members know the REALITY of the new birth as set forth in John 1:12, 13 and 3:1—18.

The Way of Water Baptism:—

The way of water baptism seems right to tens of thousands of people, but "the end thereof" is death. Some denominations teach that water baptism saves, that water washes away sins, and such churches have literally thousands of members who have been baptized (in the name of Jesus or some other formula) and who are trusting in their baptism to get them to heaven—but it will not!

Only THE BLOOD OF JESUS can wash away sins, *"and WITHOUT shedding of blood is no remission"* (Heb. 9:22). I John 1:7 tells us, "The

229

blood of Jesus Christ (God's) Son, *cleanseth us from ALL SIN.*" I Peter 1:18, 19 declares that we are not redeemed "with *corruptible* things, as silver and gold . . . *but with the precious BLOOD OF CHRIST, as of a lamb without blemish and without spot.*"

> "There is a fountain filled with blood
>   Drawn from Immanuel's veins;
> And sinners, plunged beneath *that* flood,
>   Lose all their guilty stains."

I believe *every Christian* should follow Christ in baptism—yes indeed I do. I have been baptized in water—in the name of the Father, Son, and Holy Ghost according to God's Word; but that did not save me, it did not *help* to save me, nor did it make me *any better saved!* I was baptized in water—not to BE saved, but because I was *already* saved.

The Way of Self-Righteousness: —

There are many people who believe that if they live "a good life" they can work their way to heaven. They pay their honest debts, they do not drink, they provide well for their families and give to charitable causes. They attend Sunday school and church every Sunday. Such an exemplary life, they think, prepares them for heaven —but they are mistaken. They may have done everything but the ONE thing needful—the new birth. Regardless of how honest, upright, and charitable a life may be, Jesus plainly declared, *"EXCEPT a man be born again,* he cannot see the kingdom of God!" (John 3:3). That settles it, regardless of what preachers preach or what men believe. Good works — self-righteousness — will not provide a passport to heaven. Isaiah declares, *"We are all as an unclean thing, and ALL our righteousnesses are as FILTHY RAGS!"* (Isa. 64:6). Paul wrote to the believers in Corinth, "Of Him (God) are ye *in Christ Jesus,* who of God is made unto us *wisdom, and RIGHTEOUSNESS, and sanctification, and redemption"* (I Cor. 1:30).

The Way of Living By the Golden Rule: —

Many people believe that if they treat their fellowman as they would like to be treated, that is *surely ENOUGH* — but not so! Jesus said, "Whatsoever ye would that men should do to you, do ye even so to them" (Matt. 7:12), and we sin when we wrong our fellowman; but *ALL sin is against GOD,* and when we are right with God we will treat others as we would like to be treated. Therefore living by the "golden rule" has never saved anyone, and never will. "For BY GRACE are ye saved through FAITH; and that not of yourselves: it is the gift of God: NOT OF WORKS, lest any man should boast" (Eph. 2:8, 9).

The Way of Keeping the Law: —

Many dear people still do not seem to realize

231

that "Christ is the END of the law for righteousness to every one that BELIEVETH" (Rom. 10:4).
Some preachers *preach* "law-keeping," others try
to mix law and grace. This is gross and dangerous
error. The law never saved anyone, it never could
save anyone—and even if it *could, no mortal* has
ever KEPT the law! Only the Lord Jesus Christ
could—and did—keep the law.

The law was not *given* to save. The law with
all of its rituals pointed to the coming of the Lord
Jesus, the Lamb of God, Saviour of sinners. The
Word of God is clear in declaring that the law
never saved, nor can it save today:

"By the deeds of the law there shall NO FLESH
be justified in His sight: for by the law is the
knowledge of sin. But now the righteousness of
God *without* the law is manifested, being witnessed by the law and the prophets; even the
righteousness of God which is by faith of Jesus
Christ unto all and upon all them that believe:
for there is no difference: FOR ALL HAVE
SINNED, and come short of the glory of God;
being justified freely by His grace through the
redemption that is in Christ Jesus: whom God
hath set forth to be a propitiation through faith
in His blood, to declare His righteousness for the
remission of sins that are past, through the forbearance of God; to declare, I say, at this time
His righteousness: that He might be JUST, and
the JUSTIFIER of him which believeth in Jesus.

Where is boasting then? It is excluded. By what law? of works? Nay: but by the law of FAITH. Therefore we conclude that A MAN IS JUSTIFIED BY FAITH WITHOUT THE DEEDS OF THE LAW" (Rom. 3:20—28).

In James 2:10 we are told that "whosoever shall keep the whole law, *and yet offend in ONE POINT, he is guilty of ALL!"* Only the Lord Jesus Christ kept the law perfectly. He satisfied every jot and tittle of the law. Therefore, "What the law *could NOT do,* in that it was weak through the flesh, God sending His own Son in the likeness of sinful flesh, and for sin, condemned sin in the flesh: that the righteousness of the law might be fulfilled in us, who walk not after the flesh, but after the Spirit" (Rom. 8:3, 4).

The Narrow Way

There are *many* "WAYS," but there is *only ONE WAY* TO HEAVEN—the JESUS way! This way is narrow—there is no room for anyone or anything but *Jesus.* We are not saved through His finished work *plus "religion,"* or plus *baptism,* or plus *joining a church,* or plus *living a good life,* or *living by the "golden rule,"* or *keeping the law.* We are saved through faith in the finished work of Jesus—*plus NOTHING.* He is the WAY, the TRUTH, and the LIFE. No man can come to God except through Him (John 14:6).

To the Corinthians Paul wrote: "Ye see your

calling, brethren, how that not many wise men after the flesh, not many mighty, not many noble, are called: but God hath chosen the foolish things of the world to confound the wise; and God hath chosen the weak things of the world to confound the things which are mighty; and base things of the world, and things which are despised, hath God chosen, yea, and things which are not, to bring to nought things that are: that no flesh should glory in His presence. But *OF HIM are ye in CHRIST JESUS, who of God is made unto us wisdom, and righteousness, and sanctification, and REDEMPTION:* that, according as it is written, He that glorieth, let him glory in the Lord" (I Cor. 1:26—31).

Hear Paul's words to the Colossian believers: "In HIM (Christ) dwelleth all the fulness of the Godhead bodily, and *ye are COMPLETE IN HIM*, which is the head of all principality and power" (Col. 2:9, 10).

Jesus saves us when we believe with the heart and confess Him as our Saviour. *I KNOW, because that is what I did, and He saved ME!* God's Word declares, "If thou shalt *confess with thy mouth* the Lord Jesus, and shalt *believe in thine heart* that God hath raised Him from the dead, THOU SHALT BE SAVED. For *with the heart man believeth* unto righteousness; and *with the mouth confession is made unto salvation*" (Rom. 10:9, 10).

234

Now notice: "Whosoever shall *call upon the name of the LORD* shall be saved" (Rom. 10:13). This does not say "whosoever shall join a church," or "whosoever is baptized and lives a good life." It is whosoever shall *call upon Jesus,* in faith believing. Of course, when we trust Jesus and are saved we *will* join a Bible-believing church, we will live a good life, and we will follow Christ in baptism—but we will do these things *because we ARE saved,* not in order to *BE saved.*

TWIN TREES

"Beware of false prophets, which come to you in sheep's clothing, but inwardly they are ravening wolves. Ye shall know them by their fruits. Do men gather grapes of thorns, or figs of thistles? Even so every good tree bringeth forth good fruit; but a corrupt tree bringeth forth evil fruit. A good tree cannot bring forth evil fruit, neither can a corrupt tree bring forth good fruit. Every tree that bringeth not forth good fruit is hewn down, and cast into the fire. Wherefore by their fruits ye shall know them" (Matt. 7:15—20).

The *"corrupt tree"* here represents ministers of the devil, false teachers who cannot bring forth good fruit because their hearts are evil. They preach for fame and fortune, to make a name for themselves, to build a great congregation from the numerical standpoint. They preach to satisfy man, not to bring glory to God and add souls

235

to His Church.

The *"good tree"* represents God's preachers, the preachers of righteousness. They bring forth good fruit because they have the Holy Spirit dwelling in their hearts. They preach and teach the Word of God, and bear *the fruit of the Spirit* which is "love, joy, peace, longsuffering, gentleness, goodness, faith, meekness, temperance" (Gal. 5:22, 23).

The CORRUPT Tree

"Beware of false prophets, which come to you in sheep's clothing, but inwardly they are ravening wolves." A false preacher is more dangerous and deadly than a rattlesnake or an atomic bomb! The snake's venom can kill the body but it cannot touch the soul. The atomic bomb can also destroy the body, but the most powerful explosive on earth cannot destroy the soul! A *false preacher* can destroy your soul and cause you to spend eternity in hell. You see, the devil does not care how faithfully you attend church—*just as long as you do not hear THE PURE GOSPEL preached!* Satan takes great joy in sending folks to hell from the pew of a fashionable church. The ministers of Satan may preach enough *truth* to be misleading—i. e., they can give Scripture for what they teach, but they take the Scripture out of its setting and wrongly divide it.

Jesus spoke of these men as "wolves in sheep's clothing"—outwardly seeming to be one thing, while inwardly they are another. Pretending to be ministers of the Gospel, they are actually ministers of Satan, ordained of him and preaching his "gospel." Paul describes them as "false apostles, deceitful workers, transforming themselves into the apostles of Christ. *And no marvel*—for SATAN HIMSELF is *transformed into an angel of light.* Therefore it is no great thing if his ministers also be *transformed as the ministers of righteousness;* whose end shall be according to their works" (II Cor. 11:13—15).

Paul, inspired of the Spirit, warned Timothy, "In the latter times some shall depart from the faith, giving heed to seducing spirits, and doctrines of devils; *speaking lies in hypocrisy; having their conscience seared with a hot iron*" (I Tim. 4:1, 2).

The Lord Jesus warned that *we are to "BE-WARE"* of these false teachers and ministers of Satan. Wherever we see a sign bearing the inscription *"Beware!"* we know there is danger beyond the warning sign, and if we disregard the warning we do so at our own risk and we may well suffer for it! The same is true of all who fail to heed the "BEWARE!" of Jesus concerning false prophets—and the suffering that follows will be *an ETERNITY in hell!*

God's Word also warns us to beware "of evil workers" (Phil. 3:2). We are warned to beware of "the tradition of men" (Col. 2:8). We are warned to beware "of the leaven of the Pharisees," which is hypocrisy (Matt. 16:6; Luke 12:1). We are warned to beware of "the error of the wicked" (II Pet. 3:17). All of these things are connected, either directly or indirectly, with the warning Jesus gave concerning false prophets, and there are many more passages concerning these ministers of Satan.

Even in the Old Testament days there were false prophets. Solomon, the man of wisdom, said, "He that speaketh TRUTH sheweth forth righteousness: but a *FALSE witness* deceit" (Prov. 12:17). "A *false* witness shall not be unpunished, and he that *speaketh LIES* shall not escape" (Prov. 19:5).

Hear what God declared about false prophets and false witnesses as He spoke through Jeremiah:

"The land is full of adulterers; for because of swearing the land mourneth; the pleasant places of the wilderness are dried up, and their course is evil, and their force is not right. *For BOTH PROPHET AND PRIEST are profane;* yea, *in my house have I found their wickedness. . . .* Wherefore their way shall be unto them as slippery ways in the darkness: they shall be driven on, and fall therein: for I will bring evil upon them, even the year of their visitation. . . .

"And I have seen folly in the prophets of Samaria; they prophesied in Baal, and caused my people Israel to err. I have seen also in the prophets of Jerusalem an horrible thing: They commit adultery, and walk in lies: they strengthen also the hands of evildoers, that none doth return from his wickedness: *they are all of them unto me as Sodom, and the inhabitants thereof as Gomorrah.* . . . Behold, I will feed them with wormwood, and make them drink the water of gall: for *from the prophets of Jerusalem is profaneness gone forth into all the land.* . . .

"*Hearken not* unto the words of the prophets that prophesy unto you: they make you vain: *they speak a vision of their own heart, and NOT OUT OF THE MOUTH OF THE LORD.* . . . I have heard what the prophets said, that prophesy *lies* in my name, saying, I have dreamed, I have dreamed. How long shall this be in the heart of the prophets that prophesy lies? Yea, they are prophets of *the deceit of their own heart; which think to cause my people to forget my name* by their dreams which they tell every man to his neighbour, as their fathers have forgotten my name for Baal. The prophet that *hath a dream,* let him *tell* a dream; and *he that hath MY WORD, let him SPEAK my Word faithfully!* . . . Is not my Word like as a fire? . . . and like a hammer that breaketh the rock in pieces?

"Therefore, behold, *I am AGAINST the prophets . . . that steal my words every one from his neighbour. . . . Behold, I am AGAINST them that prophesy false dreams . . . and do tell them, and cause my people to err BY THEIR LIES,* and by their lightness; *yet I sent them NOT, nor com-*

239

manded them. Therefore they shall not profit this people at all" (Jer. 23:10—32 in part).

The dirtiest, most contemptible thief THIS SIDE OF HELL is a lying preacher, one who stands before the people and professes to preach the Gospel—but preaches false doctrine instead! God pity that preacher when he stands before the judgment bar to give an account for the deeds done in this life!

How can we recognize these false prophets? Certainly not by outward appearance, because they *dress* like true prophets, they may even *speak* like true prophets. According to the words of Jesus in our text, *we can know them "BY THEIR FRUITS."* How can we recognize the "fruit" of a true prophet? Again the answer is found in the Word of God. In I Peter 2:6 we read, "Wherefore also it is contained in the Scripture, Behold, I lay in Sion a chief corner stone, elect, precious: and *he that believeth on Him shall not be CONFOUNDED (or, CONFUSED)."*

John the Beloved also tells us, "Ye have an unction from the Holy One, and *ye know ALL THINGS. . . .* But the anointing which ye have received of Him abideth in you, and *ye need not that any man teach you:* but as the same anointing *teacheth you of ALL THINGS,* and is truth, and is no lie, and even as it hath taught you, ye shall abide in Him" (I John 2:20, 27).

Born again believers are not confused by false

teachers. The *Author* of the Holy Scriptures dwells within our hearts and *He, the Holy Spirit, TEACHES us* the truths of God's Word, He *LEADS us* into paths of righteousness, He *SEALS us* until the day of redemption. This is clearly pointed out in the following passages:

"Ye are not in the *flesh,* but *in the Spirit,* if so be that the Spirit of God dwell in you. *Now if any man have NOT the Spirit of Christ, HE IS NONE OF HIS. . . .* For as many as are *led* by the Spirit of God, they are the sons of God. *. . . The Spirit Himself beareth witness with our spirit, that we ARE the children of God"* (Rom. 8:9, 14, 16).

"The Lord is my Shepherd; I shall not want. *. . . He LEADETH me in the paths of righteousness* for His name's sake" (Psalm 23:1, 3).

In John 16:12—15 Jesus said to His disciples, "I have yet many things to say unto you, but ye cannot bear them now. *Howbeit when HE, THE SPIRIT OF TRUTH, is come, He will guide you into ALL truth:* for He shall not speak of Himself; but whatsoever He shall hear, that shall He speak: and He will shew you things to come. He shall glorify me: for He shall receive of mine, and shall shew it unto you. All things that the Father hath are mine: therefore said I, that *He shall take of mine, and shall shew it unto you.*"

Then in Ephesians 4:30 Paul warns, *"Grieve not the Holy Spirit of God, whereby ye are*

SEALED unto the day of redemption!"

When God's man preaches God's Word, the Holy Spirit in the heart of the believer witnesses with the Holy Spirit in the heart of the preacher— and *if there IS no witnessing of the Spirit* you can rest assured that you are listening to a minister of Satan. And regardless of who that minister may be—your pastor, a visiting evangelist, a radio preacher—do not keep listening just out of curiosity. That can be dangerous. Read your Bible, or find a man of God to listen to. Give no support whatsoever to a false prophet, lest you become "partaker of his evil deeds" (II John 11).

I John 4:1—4 warns, "Beloved, believe not *every* spirit, but *try the spirits whether they are of GOD:* because *MANY false prophets* are gone out into the world. Hereby know ye the Spirit of God: Every spirit that confesseth that *Jesus Christ is come in the flesh* is of God: And every spirit that *confesseth NOT* that Jesus Christ is come in the flesh *is NOT of God:* and this is that spirit of antichrist, whereof ye have heard that it should come; and even now already is it in the world. *YE ARE OF GOD, little children, and have overcome them: because greater is He that is in YOU, than he that is in THE WORLD!"*

Also in I John 2:18, 19 we read, "Little children, it is the last time: and as ye have heard that antichrist shall come, *EVEN NOW are there many*

242

antichrists; whereby we know that it is the last time. *They went out FROM us, but they were not OF us;* for if they had been *OF us,* they would no doubt have continued *WITH us:* but *they WENT OUT, that they might be made manifest that they were not all of us."*

There are many, many more Scriptures which deal with false preachers and teachers, and their message of lies, but time and space allotted to this message will not permit us to deal with all such passages. We have given a sufficient number to establish the fact that false prophets were on earth even in the days when Jesus walked among men—and there *will be* false prophets until He comes again and puts down all evil. *The greatest of ALL false prophets, the Antichrist, is yet to come.* He will appear after the Rapture of the Church. (Study Revelation chapters 13 and 14. Also read Revelation 19:20 and 20:10.)

Some Christians say, "I think we should be nice to everyone, regardless of what they preach or teach." Others (also mistakenly) ask, "If people are sincere in what they believe, is not *their* religion as good as any *other* religion?" No! Emphatically *No!* In the first place, Christians do not have *"religion"*—we have *salvation.* "Religion" is simply worshipping someone, or some thing. *Christianity is POSSESSING CHRIST BY FAITH!*

According to God's Word, His children are

forbidden to accept false preachers or have any fellowship with them:

"Look to yourselves, that we lose not those things which we have wrought, but that we *receive a FULL reward.* Whosoever transgresseth, and abideth not in the doctrine of Christ, hath not God. He that abideth in the doctrine of Christ, he hath both the Father and the Son. *If there come any unto you, and BRING NOT this doctrine, receive him not into your house, neither bid him God speed: For HE THAT BIDDETH HIM GOD SPEED IS PARTAKER OF HIS EVIL DEEDS"* (II John 8—11).

Yes, we shall know them by their fruits—and *"a CORRUPT tree" CANNOT bring forth good fruit* (Matt. 7:18).

The GOOD Tree

"Even so, *every GOOD tree* bringeth forth *good fruit . . ."* (Matt. 7:17). These, of course, are God's preachers, called, ordained, and sent of God, and *they preach CHRIST*—not "religion," not "program," but Christ, and Him crucified:

"Therefore seeing we have this ministry, as we have received mercy, we faint not; but have renounced the hidden things of dishonesty, not walking in craftiness, nor handling the Word of God deceitfully; but by manifestation of the truth commending ourselves to every man's conscience in the sight of God. But if our Gospel be hid,

244

it is hid to them that are lost: in whom the god of this world hath blinded the minds of them which believe not, lest the light of the glorious Gospel of Christ, who is the image of God, should shine unto them. *For we preach NOT OUR-SELVES, BUT CHRIST JESUS THE LORD; and ourselves your servants for Jesus' sake. For God, who commanded the light to shine out of dark-ness, hath shined in our hearts, to give the light of the knowledge of the glory of God in the face of Jesus Christ"* (II Cor. 4:1−6).

It is through the preaching of His ministers that God saves souls: "For the preaching of the cross is to them that perish foolishness; but unto us which are saved it is the power of God. For it is written, I will destroy the wisdom of the wise, and will bring to nothing the understanding of the prudent. Where is the wise? Where is the scribe? Where is the disputer of this world? Hath not God made foolish the wisdom of this world? *For after that in the wisdom of God the world by wisdom KNEW NOT God, it pleased God by THE FOOLISHNESS OF PREACHING to save them that believe"* (I Cor. 1:18−21).

The Apostle Paul declared, *"Whosoever shall CALL upon the name of the Lord shall be SAVED"*—and then explained that it is God's plan in this Day of Grace to save souls through the preaching of men whom God calls and sends:

"How then shall they CALL on Him in whom

245

they have not BELIEVED? And how shall they BELIEVE in Him of whom they have not HEARD? And how shall they HEAR without a PREACHER? And how shall they PREACH, except they be SENT? As it is written, How beautiful are the feet of them that preach THE GOSPEL OF PEACE, and bring glad tidings of good things! . . . So then FAITH cometh by HEARING, and hearing by THE WORD OF GOD" (Rom. 10:13—17).

In II Timothy 4:1—5 Paul gave a solemn charge to young Timothy—a charge that should be read over and over again by God's preachers today:

"I charge thee therefore *before God, and the Lord Jesus Christ,* who shall judge the quick and the dead at His appearing and His kingdom: *PREACH THE WORD!* Be instant in season, out of season. *Reprove, rebuke, exhort with all longsuffering and doctrine.* For the time will come when they will not endure sound doctrine; but after their own lusts shall they heap to themselves teachers, having itching ears; and they shall turn away their ears from the truth, and shall be turned unto fables. *But WATCH THOU IN ALL THINGS, endure afflictions, do the work of an evangelist, MAKE FULL PROOF OF THY MINISTRY!"*

God grant that I may never compromise His Word! God give me grace to preach Jesus Christ— crucified, buried, risen, coming again "according

246

to the Scriptures." I had rather die today than fail God in being true to His holy Word. With all my heart I want to be like Paul—*"determined not to know any thing among you, save JESUS CHRIST, and Him crucified"* (I Cor. 2:2).

TWIN FRUITS

". . . Do men gather grapes of thorns, or figs of thistles? Even so *every GOOD tree* bringeth forth *good fruit;* but *a CORRUPT tree* bringeth forth *evil fruit.* A good tree *cannot* bring forth *evil* fruit, neither can a corrupt tree bring forth *good* fruit. Every tree that bringeth not forth good fruit is hewn down, and cast into the fire. Wherefore by their *fruits* ye shall know them" (Matt. 7:16—20).

These are the words of Jesus. When we study His sermons and parables we find that He always preached in down-to-earth language, words so simple that a child could understand them. He talked of the sower and the seed, the lilies of the fields, the sparrow, the grass, sheep and shepherds, old and new garments. Every lesson He taught could be easily understood by all who heard Him. There is absolutely no excuse for people going to hell after hearing or reading the words of Jesus, for He came to earth to save sinners and He made God's truth so simple that sinners could know the way to heaven without using a dictionary to look up the words He used!

In our present passage Jesus asked a simple question: *"Do men gather grapes of thorns, or figs of thistles?"* Even today Palestine is noted for its vineyards and fig orchards. The vineyard and the fig tree are often mentioned in Scripture, and Jesus used such references more than once in His teaching. (See Matthew 20:1 and 21:33 for example.) Certainly the people to whom He was speaking knew that one did not find *grapes* growing on a thorn bush, nor did figs grow on thistles. It is just as impossible, then, that good fruit come from an evil tree or bad fruit come from a good tree—and the comparison is very meaningful when applied to ministers of God contrasted with ministers of Satan!

"Even so, every GOOD tree bringeth forth good FRUIT." There is no "perhaps" or "maybe" about it: every good tree bears good fruit simply because it IS a good tree! By like token, a true minister of the Gospel preaches *the pure, unadulterated truth* of the Gospel because he is God's minister and he cannot, will not, preach a corrupt message adding to or taking from the Word of God. A true minister will not take Scripture out of its setting in order to prove a denominational point or please a church official. God's true servant (represented by the "good tree") will bring forth good fruit because *"HIS SEED* (the Word of God) *remaineth in him"* (I John 3:9). Good seed produces *good fruit.*

"A CORRUPT tree bringeth forth EVIL fruit."
There is no excuse for born again people support-
ing a minister of Satan—a liberal or modernist.
True Christians can know whether or not the
preacher they support is bringing forth *good* fruit,
or *evil* fruit. Are souls being saved where you
attend church? Notice—I did not ask if people
are "joining" your church, but are they being
SAVED? God's Word is the power of God unto
salvation, and when His Word is preached in all
of its purity and power SOULS ARE SAVED!

God promises, "As the rain cometh down, and
the snow from heaven, and returneth not thither,
but watereth the earth, and maketh it bring forth
and bud, that it may give seed to the sower, and
bread to the eater: *SO SHALL MY WORD BE
that goeth forth out of my mouth! It shall NOT
return unto me void, but IT SHALL ACCOM-
PLISH THAT WHICH I PLEASE, and it shall
PROSPER in the thing whereto I sent it"* (Isa.
55:10, 11). Therefore, when God's man preaches
God's Word, souls will be saved—there is no question about it.

On the other hand, *a "CORRUPT tree" cannot*
bring forth good fruit. The false preacher may
look like a true minister, he may, up to a certain
point, *sound* like a true minister. He may read
from the Scriptures and mix some degree of truth
with the error he preaches: *but he CANNOT
bring forth fruit that will glorify God and add*

souls to God's kingdom! In the words of Jesus, "A corrupt tree bringeth forth *evil fruit* . . . neither *can* a corrupt tree bring forth *good* fruit."

Also by the words of Jesus we know that there will be people at the judgment who will attempt to justify themselves before God by reminding Him that they preached, cast out demons, and did *many wonderful works IN HIS NAME.* They expect to enter heaven through their "good works." I believe there will be Sunday school teachers, preachers, evangelists, deacons, and other advocates of good works who will hear the sad words, "I never knew you! Depart from me, ye that work iniquity!" (Matt. 7:21—23). These corrupt trees will be cut down and cast into the fire— *hell fire,* if you please.

Therefore (because a *good* tree cannot bear *evil fruit* and a *corrupt tree* cannot bear *good* fruit) the *fruit* found on a tree determines *the STATUS of the tree—GOOD or BAD.*

"By their fruits ye shall know them." When we drive through the country and see apples on a tree, we know without question that we are looking at an *apple tree.* By like token we know that a *peach* tree bears peaches, a *pear* tree bears pears, and so on. By their *fruits* we can easily recognize the trees.

So it is in the spiritual realm. A minister who does not bear fruit evidenced by soul-winning, pointing men to Jesus through the pure Gospel of God's grace, is ordained of the devil. A minister who denies the virgin birth, the blood atonement, the necessity of the new birth, the second coming of Jesus and the literality of hell is certainly not ordained of God. He is bringing forth corrupt fruit and he will suffer according to his corruptness—yes, in a literal and everlasting hell!

II Peter chapter 2 describes these "corrupt trees," these apostate teachers, and tells us how we may know them. They "bring in *damnable heresies*, even denying the Lord that bought them and bring upon themselves swift destruction. And *MANY shall FOLLOW their pernicious ways;* by reason of whom the Way of Truth shall be evil spoken of. And through covetousness shall they with feigned words *make merchandise of you:* whose judgment now of a long time lingereth not, and their damnation slumbereth not.

"For if God spared not the angels that sinned, but cast them down to hell, and delivered them into chains of darkness, to be reserved unto judgment; and spared not the old world, but saved Noah the eighth person, a preacher of righteousness, bringing in the flood upon the world of the ungodly; and turning the cities of Sodom and Gomorrha into ashes condemned them with an overthrow, making them an ensample unto those that after should live ungodly; and delivered just Lot, vexed with the filthy conversation of the wicked. (For that righteous man dwelling among them, in seeing and hearing, vexed his righteous soul from day to day with their unlawful deeds;) the Lord knoweth how to deliver the godly out of temptations, and to reserve the unjust unto the day of judgment to be punished: but chiefly them that walk after the flesh in the lust of uncleanness, and despise government.

"Presumptuous are they, selfwilled, they are not afraid to speak evil of dignities. Whereas angels, which are greater in power and might, bring not railing accusation against them before the Lord. But these, as natural brute beasts, made to be taken and destroyed, speak evil of the things that they understand not; and shall utterly perish in their own corruption; and shall receive the reward of unrighteousness, as they that count it pleasure to riot in the day time. Spots they are, and blemishes, sporting themselves with their own deceivings while they feast with you; having eyes full of adultery, and that cannot cease from sin; beguiling unstable souls: an heart they have exercised with covetous practices; cursed children: which have forsaken the right way, and are gone astray, following the way of Balaam the son of Bosor, who loved the wages of unrighteousness; but was rebuked for his iniquity: the dumb ass speaking with man's voice forbad the madness of the prophet.

"THESE ARE WELLS WITHOUT WATER, CLOUDS THAT ARE CARRIED WITH A TEM-

PEST; to whom the mist of darkness is reserved for ever! For when they speak great swelling words of vanity, they allure through the lusts of the flesh, through much wantonness, those that were clean escaped from them who live in error. While they promise them liberty, they themselves are the servants of corruption: for of whom a man is overcome, of the same is he brought in bondage.

"For if after they have escaped the pollutions of the world through the knowledge of the Lord and Saviour Jesus Christ, they are again entangled therein, and overcome, the latter end is worse with them than the beginning. For it had been better for them not to have known the way of righteousness, than, after they have known it, to turn from the holy commandment delivered unto them.

"But it is happened unto them according to the true proverb, The dog is turned to his own vomit again; and the sow that was washed to her wallowing in the mire" (II Pet. 2:1—22).

Be not deceived, beloved—these are not preachers who were once saved and then lost their salvation! These are men who were exposed to the Gospel—but they did not receive it in their hearts. They know the Way of Truth—but they refuse to follow it. Furthermore, they lead others into error and hell—*"MANY shall follow their pernicious ways!"*

TWIN BUILDERS

"Therefore whosoever heareth these sayings of mine, and doeth them, I will liken him unto a wise man, which built his house upon a rock: and the rain descended, and the floods came, and the winds blew, and beat upon that house; and it fell not: for it was founded upon a rock.

"And every one that heareth these sayings of mine, and doeth them not, shall be likened unto a foolish man, which built his house upon the sand: and the rain descended, and the floods came, and the winds blew, and beat upon that house; and it fell: and great was the fall of it" (Matt. 7:24—27).

Our twins in this passage are "builders," and again they are opposites, not identical twins. Jesus speaks of one builder as "a *wise* man" and the other He calls "a *foolish* man."

The Wise Man

Two things characterize this man: (1) *"Whosoever HEARETH these sayings* (the Word of God) . . ."* and (2) *"DOETH them."*

God's Word is the only message on earth that reveals God's saving grace and keeping power. Everything we know about God's love, mercy, and salvation, we know because of His Word, and the only way for any sinner to find help is to *hear* the Word of God.

The unbeliever is dead in trespasses and sin

(Eph. 2:1). His mind is blinded by the god of this world (II Cor. 4:3,4). He is led about by the devil, walking "according to the course of this world . . . fulfilling the desires of the flesh and of the mind" (Eph. 2:2,3). In other words, the unbeliever is dead, blind, held captive by the devil, and *he needs help.* That is where the Word of God comes in.

Man is in utter darkness until he *hears the WORD OF GOD*—and *does what the Word commands.* The entrance of the Word gives light (Psalm 119:130). "God is light, and in Him is no darkness at all" (I John 1:5). When a sinner hears—*really HEARS*—the Word, he sees his lost condition, realizes his need of a Saviour, and the light of the Word leads him to Jesus. Hearing the Word brings saving faith (and *without* faith it is impossible to please God—Heb. 11:6). The only possible way for an unbeliever to exercise saving faith is to hear the Word (Rom. 10:17). Faith brings saving grace, and the grace that saves also *teaches* us that, "denying ungodliness and worldly lusts, we should live soberly, righteously, and godly, in this present world; looking for that blessed hope, and the glorious appearing of the great God and our Saviour Jesus Christ; who gave Himself for us, that He might redeem us from all iniquity, and purify unto Himself a peculiar people, zealous of good works" (Tit. 2:11—14).

So we see that the Word of God, after salvation, becomes a light to our pathway (Psalm 119:105), showing us how to live *after* we are saved. The Word is *the SEED* that bursts forth *into LIFE ETERNAL* when we hear and literally appropriate the Word. James 1:21 tells us that we are to "receive with meekness the *engrafted Word*" which is able to save our souls. I Peter 1:23 speaks of the Word as the *"incorruptible seed"* that brings the new birth.

Remember, the *"wise* man" is the man who *HEARS and DOES* the sayings of Jesus: "Verily, verily, I say unto you, *HE THAT HEARETH MY WORD, and believeth on Him that sent me, hath everlasting life, and SHALL NOT come into condemnation; but is passed from death unto life"* (John 5:24).

The Foolish Man

This is the man who hears with the ear, but does not hear with the heart. In other words, he does not really *believe* what he hears. He is exposed to the Word of God, but refuses to *receive* it, refuses to *do* what the Word tells him to do. Jesus tells of such people. In Matthew 13:10—16 we read:

"The disciples came, and said unto Him, Why speakest thou unto them in parables? He answered and said unto them, Because it is given *unto YOU* to know the mysteries of the kingdom of

256

heaven, but *to THEM it is NOT given.* For whosoever hath not, from him shall be taken away even that he hath. *Therefore speak I to them in parables: because they seeing SEE NOT; and hearing they HEAR NOT, NEITHER DO THEY UNDERSTAND.*

"And in them is fulfilled the prophecy of E-saias, which saith, By hearing ye shall hear, and shall not understand; and seeing ye shall see, and shall not perceive: For this people's heart is waxed gross, and their ears are dull of hearing, and their eyes they have closed; lest at any time they should see with their eyes and hear with their ears, and should understand with their heart, and should be converted, and I should heal them.

"But *blessed are YOUR eyes, for THEY SEE: and YOUR ears, for they HEAR.*"

The men of whom Jesus spoke in this passage claimed to be custodians of the Word of God. They knew Moses, they knew Abraham. They claimed to be the *children* of Abraham. They were well acquainted with the Mosaic Law—on several occasions they even accused Jesus of *breaking* the law. But this was *mental* knowledge— a knowledge of the head, not of the heart. It would have been better for them if they had never known the Old Testament Scriptures than, having known them, to reject the Christ of whom their Old Testament prophets wrote—and that is exactly what they did. They closed their eyes, stopped their ears, and refused to believe that Jesus was the Christ of God, their promised Messiah.

How about YOU, dear reader? YOU have heard the sayings of Jesus in this message—and no doubt you have heard them many times before. You have heard:

"Ye MUST be born again" (John 3:3—7).

"Except ye repent, ye shall all . . . perish" (Luke 13:3, 5).

"By GRACE are ye saved THROUGH FAITH; and that not of yourselves: it is the gift of God" (Eph. 2:8).

"Not by works of righteousness which we have done, but *according to HIS MERCY He saved us,* by the washing of regeneration, and renewing of the Holy Ghost" (Tit. 3:5).

". . . Him that cometh to me *I will in no wise cast out"* (John 6:37).

"WHOSOEVER shall call upon the name of the Lord shall be saved" (Rom. 10:13).

"The Lord is not . . . willing *that ANY should perish* (and that includes YOU), but that ALL should come to repentance" (II Pet. 3:9).

You have heard these precious words of warning and promise—*but what have you DONE about it?* Are you born again? If you are, then you are like the wise man who built his house upon a rock. If you are *not* saved, now is the time to *be* saved and begin this moment to build your spiritual house upon the Rock, Christ Jesus. Before another day—even another hour—you may be in eternity. Be WISE. Trust Jesus as your Saviour this moment!

TWIN FOUNDATIONS

"Therefore whosoever heareth these sayings of mine, and doeth them, I will liken him unto a wise man, which built his house upon a rock. And the rain descended, and the floods came, and the winds blew, and beat upon that house; and it fell not: for it was founded upon a rock. And everyone that heareth these sayings of mine, and doeth them not, shall be likened unto a foolish man, which built his house upon the sand: and the rain descended, and the floods came, and the winds blew, and beat upon that house; and it fell: and great was the fall of it" (Matt. 7:24—27).

The "ROCK" is the Lord Jesus Christ. This truth is clearly taught in the Scriptures. In I Corinthians 10:4 the Apostle Paul declared, "They (the Israelite fathers) drank of that spiritual Rock that followed them: *and that Rock was CHRIST.*"

Jesus Himself declared, *"The STONE which the builders rejected, the same is become the head of the corner: . . .* Whosoever shall *fall on this Stone* shall be broken: but *on whomsoever it shall fall,* it will grind him to powder!" (Matt. 21:42—44).

Christ as the Stone is revealed in a threefold way:

(1) *To ISRAEL* He was a "stumblingstone." Paul declared, "We preach Christ crucified—*unto the Jews a stumblingblock . . .*" (I Cor. 1:23). In Romans 9:32, 33 Paul said of Israel, ". . . They stumbled at that stumblingstone. As it is written, Behold, I lay in Sion *a Stumblingstone and Rock of offence:* and whosoever believeth on Him shall not be ashamed." Peter speaks of Christ as *the "Chief Cornerstone . . . a Stone of stumbling,* and *a Rock of offence,* even to them which stumble at the Word, being disobedient . . ." (I Pet. 2:6—8).

(2) *To the CHURCH* Christ is the *solid Foundation,* "for other foundation can no man lay than that is laid, *which is JESUS CHRIST"* (I Cor. 3:11). When Christ asked His disciples, "Whom do men say that I the Son of man am?" they answered, "Some say that thou art John the Baptist: some, Elias; and others, Jeremias, or one of the prophets." He then asked them, *"But whom say YE that I am?"* and Simon Peter replied, *"THOU ART THE CHRIST, the Son of the living God!"* Jesus then said: "Blessed art thou, Simon Bar-jona: for flesh and blood hath not revealed it unto thee, but my Father which is in heaven. And I say also unto thee, That thou art Peter, and *upon this ROCK I will build my Church;* and the gates of hell shall not prevail against it" (Matt. 16:13—18).

To the believers at Ephesus Paul wrote, "Now therefore ye are no more strangers and foreigners, but fellowcitizens with the saints, and of the household of God; and are *built upon the FOUNDATION of the apostles and prophets, JESUS CHRIST HIMSELF BEING THE CHIEF CORNER STONE; in whom all the building fitly framed together groweth unto an holy temple in the Lord: in whom ye also are builded together for AN HABITATION OF GOD through the Spirit*" (Eph. 2:19—22).

Peter speaks of Jesus as *"a LIVING STONE, disallowed indeed of men, but chosen of God, and precious."* He speaks of believers as *"lively stones* . . . built up a spiritual house, an holy priesthood, to offer up spiritual sacrifices, *acceptable to God by Jesus Christ*" (I Pet. 2:4,5).

(3) *To the GENTILE WORLD POWERS*, Christ is the *smiting Stone*, for He will in the end *completely CRUSH* the Gentile powers. Daniel wrote of this as the Stone "cut out without hands," the Stone which smote the great image of Nebuchadnezzar's dream and broke it to pieces. "And the Stone that smote the image became a great mountain, and filled the whole earth." (Read Daniel 2:31—35.)

Israel, God's chosen nation, *stumbled* over Christ, their Messiah. The *Church* is *built* upon Christ the Rock. And one day *Gentile world dominion* will be *completely crushed and broken*

261

by Christ, the Stone cut out of the mountain without hands.

The Old Testament contains many passages which speak of "the Rock," and that Rock of the Old Testament is the Christ of the New Testament. Hear the words of Moses concerning the Rock—words inspired of God: In Deuteronomy 32:3, 4 he wrote, "I will publish the name of the Lord: ascribe ye greatness unto our God. *HE IS THE ROCK,* His work is perfect: for all His ways are judgment: a God of truth and without iniquity, just and right is He."

No statement could be plainer! God is "the Rock." His work is perfect, He is the God of truth. He is without iniquity, He is just and right. *This is the Rock* upon which the wise man built his house, the Rock upon which *you* are building if you are born again.

Some of the people in Moses' day forgot "the Rock of their salvation." They went after other gods—gods of their own making. We might call them "sand gods," for sand is nothing more than tiny rocks from which the soil is washed away. Now hear these words of warning, penned by Moses under inspiration, still applicable to us today if we turn from the solid Rock and build upon the sand:

"Jeshurun waxed fat, and kicked: thou art waxen fat, thou art grown thick, thou art covered with fatness; *then he forsook God which made*

*him, and lightly esteemed THE ROCK OF HIS
SALVATION.* They provoked Him to jealousy
with strange gods, with abominations provoked
they Him to anger. They sacrificed unto devils,
not to God; to gods whom they knew not, to
new gods that came newly up, whom your fathers
feared not. *Of the Rock that begat thee thou
art unmindful, and hast forgotten God that formed
thee.*

"And when the Lord saw it, He abhorred them,
because of the provoking of His sons, and of His
daughters. And He said, I will hide my face
from them, I will see what their end shall be:
for they are a very froward generation, children
in whom is no faith. They have moved me to
jealousy with that which is not God; they have
provoked me to anger with their vanities: and I
will move them to jealousy with those which are
not a people; I will provoke them to anger with
a foolish nation. For a fire is kindled in mine
anger, and shall burn unto the lowest hell, and
shall consume the earth with her increase, and
set on fire the foundations of the mountains. . . .

"O that they were wise, that they understood
this, that they would consider their latter end!
How should one chase a thousand, and two put
ten thousand to flight, except their Rock had sold
them, and the Lord had shut them up? For their
rock is not as our Rock, even our enemies themselves being judges. For their vine is of the vine

of Sodom, and of the fields of Gomorrah: their grapes are grapes of gall, their clusters are bitter: their wine is the poison of dragons, and the cruel venom of asps. . . .

"See now that I, even I, am He, and there is no god with me. I kill, and I make alive. I wound, and I heal: neither is there any that can deliver out of my hand. For I lift up my hand to heaven, and say, I live for ever! If I whet my glittering sword, and mine hand take hold on judgment; I will render vengeance to mine enemies, and will reward them that hate me. I will make mine arrows drunk with blood, and my sword shall devour flesh; and that with the blood of the slain and of the captives, from the beginning of revenges upon the enemy.

"Rejoice, O ye nations, with His people: for He will avenge the blood of His servants, and will render vengeance to His adversaries, and will be merciful unto His land, and to His people" (Deut. 32:15—43 in part).

Now what do we find in this passage that we may apply to our own lives today? *"Jeshurun waxed fat* (he prospered), *then HE FORSOOK GOD WHICH MADE HIM."* Israel provoked God to jealousy and then anger. This is the same God we hear so much about today, from pulpits of liberals and modernists—the "God of love." It is true that He is a God of love—*He IS love* (I John 4:8); but He is also *"a consuming FIRE"*

264

(Heb. 12:29).

God said to Jeremiah, *"I WILL UTTER MY JUDGMENTS AGAINST THEM* touching all their wickedness, who have *forsaken me,* and have *burned incense unto other gods,* and *worshipped the works of their own hands"* (Jer. 1:16). These were *God's chosen people,* a nation whom He had blessed in a peculiar and singular way; but when they forsook Him and made their own gods, He poured out His wrath upon them. Read the account in Deuteronomy again—and *tremble!* If Israel, God's chosen people, did not escape His wrath, how can *we* hope to escape if we go after other gods?

There are hundreds of thousands of idol worshippers in America today—and most of them are *church members.* They make gods of many things—business, pleasure, houses and lands, even church and denomination. Like Israel of old, these modern idolaters miss Christ altogether in their worship of "things" and "programs." God did exactly what He said He would do in dealing with Israel, and to people of our day He will do exactly what He declares in His Word.

The greatest program of idolatry this world will ever know is just ahead and will take place during the reign of the false messiah, the Antichrist. He will sit in the temple in Jerusalem announcing that he is God—and the masses will *worship* him as God; but Jesus will come and destroy the Antichrist and his system of idolatry. Therefore the most horrible judgment ever to come on earth is just ahead.

During His public ministry, Jesus told the people that all of this would happen—but they did not believe Him. Multitudes today do not believe that Antichrist will come. But *he WILL come*, just as God's Word declares, and the horrible judgment spelled out in the book of Revelation will also come upon the world. Of course, if you are saved you have nothing to worry about for you will be with Jesus in the air; but if you are *not* saved you could very well be here when Antichrist is revealed and you will go through a time of tribulation such as this world has never known. I urge you to give your heart to Jesus before it is too late.

Hear the prophetic prayer of Hannah concerning the Rock our God:

"Hannah prayed and said: My heart rejoiceth in the Lord, mine horn is exalted in the Lord; my mouth is enlarged over mine enemies because I rejoice in thy salvation. There is none holy as the Lord: for there is none beside thee: *neither is there any ROCK LIKE OUR GOD.* Talk no more so exceeding proudly; let not arrogancy come out of your mouth: for the Lord is a God of knowledge, and by Him actions are weighed. The bows of the mighty men are broken, and they that stumbled are girded with strength. They that were full have hired out themselves for bread; and they that were hungry ceased: so that the barren hath borne seven; and she that hath many children is waxed feeble. The Lord killeth, and maketh alive: He bringeth down to the grave, and bringeth up. The Lord maketh poor, and maketh rich: He bringeth low, and lifteth up. He raiseth up the poor out of the dust, and lifteth up the beggar from the dunghill, to set them among princes, and to make them inherit the throne of glory: for the pillars of the earth are the Lord's, and He hath set the world upon them" (I Sam. 2:1—8).

There is none other in earth or in heaven like our God! He exalts, He puts down. He kills, and He makes alive. God help us to see the Bible truth about our God, the Rock of our salvation!

David, a man after God's own heart, had much to say about the Rock upon which wise men build their lives. For example, in Psalm 31:1—3 he wrote, "In thee, O Lord, do I put my trust; let me never be ashamed: deliver me in thy right-eousness. Bow down thine ear to me; deliver me speedily: *be thou my strong ROCK*, for an house of defense to save me. *For thou art MY ROCK AND MY FORTRESS;* therefore for thy name's sake lead me, and guide me."

In Psalm 61:1—3 David prayed, "Hear my cry, O God; attend unto my prayer. From the end of the earth will I cry unto thee, when my heart is overwhelmed. Lead me to THE ROCK that is higher than I; for thou hast been a shelter for me, and a strong tower from the enemy."

In Psalm 71:1—3 we read, "In thee, O Lord, do I put my trust: let me never be put to confusion. Deliver me in thy righteousness, and cause me to escape: incline thine ear unto me, and save me. Be thou my strong habitation, whereunto I may continually resort: Thou hast given commandment to save me, for *thou art MY ROCK AND MY FORTRESS!*"

In Psalm 92:12—15 David wrote, "The righteous shall flourish like the palm tree: he shall grow like a cedar in Lebanon. Those that be planted in the house of the Lord shall flourish in the courts of our God. They shall still bring forth fruit in old age; they shall be fat and flourishing; to shew that the Lord is upright: *HE IS MY ROCK, and there is no unrighteousness in Him.*"

In Psalm 18:1, 2 David praised the Lord as his Deliverer: "I will love thee, *O Lord, my strength. The Lord is MY ROCK, and MY FORTRESS, and MY DELIVERER;* my God, my strength, in whom I will trust; my buckler, and the horn of my salvation, and my high tower."

Then in David's last words, recorded in II Samuel 23:1—4 we read: "Now these be the last words of David. David the son of Jesse . . . the anointed of the God of Jacob, and the sweet Psalmist of Israel, said:

"The Spirit of the Lord spake by me, and His Word was in my tongue. The God of Israel said, *THE ROCK OF ISRAEL spake to me,* He that ruleth over men must be just, ruling in the fear of God. And He shall be as the light of the morning, when the sun riseth, even a morning without clouds; as the tender grass springing out of the earth by clear shining after rain."

We might also look at a few of the men whose names are recorded in Scripture as having built their house upon the Rock. In other words, *they HEARD the Word of God and DID WHAT IT COMMANDED.*

Abel was one of the first to build upon the Rock. He knew the kind of offering God demanded and he brought such an offering, one that was acceptable unto the Lord (Gen. 4:1—4). Hebrews 11:4 tells us that it was by FAITH that Abel brought a blood offering—and where do we obtain faith? "Faith cometh by HEARING, and hearing by THE WORD OF GOD" (Rom. 10:17).

Noah was another "wise man" who built his house upon the Rock. Genesis chapter 6 records God's declaration that He would destroy the earth and every living thing on it. "But *NOAH found GRACE* in the eyes of the Lord" (Gen. 6:8), and again Hebrews 11:7 reveals that it was by FAITH that Noah found grace. Noah believed what God said: "By FAITH Noah, being warned of God of things not seen as yet, moved with fear, prepared an ark to the saving of his house; by the which he condemned the world, and became heir of the righteousness which is by faith." Noah had never seen rain, "for the Lord God had not caused it to rain upon the earth . . . but there went up a mist from the earth, and watered the whole face of the ground" (Gen. 2:5, 6). But God told Noah He was going to send a flood on the earth, and Noah *believed* what God said. He HEARD, and he OBEYED what he heard.

Abraham built his house upon the Rock, and certainly his house stood the test of time and storm. *"Abraham BELIEVED GOD, and it was counted unto him for righteousness"* (Rom. 4:3). In Genesis 12:1—4 we read where God called Abraham out of his country, into a land which God would show him, and that land would be given to Abraham and his descendants. And in Hebrews 11:8 we read, *"By FAITH* Abraham, when he was called to go out into a place which he should after receive for an inheritance, *obeyed;* and he went out, not knowing whither he went." He heard the Word of God, he believed and obeyed what he heard, "and it was counted unto him for righteousness."

Moses built his house upon the Rock, and God used him as He has used few men since the *creation* of man. Exodus chapter 3 tells of God's call to Moses from the burning bush, and in Hebrews 11:23—29 Paul tells us, "By FAITH Moses,

270

when he was born, was hid three months of his parents, because they saw he was a proper child; and they were not afraid of the king's commandment. By FAITH Moses, when he was come to years, refused to be called the son of Pharaoh's daughter; choosing rather to suffer affliction with the people of God, than to enjoy the pleasures of sin for a season; esteeming the reproach of Christ greater riches than the treasures in Egypt: for he had respect unto the recompense of the reward. By FAITH he forsook Egypt, not fearing the wrath of the king: for he endured, as seeing Him who is invisible. Through FAITH he kept the passover, and the sprinkling of blood, lest he that destroyed the first-born should touch them. By FAITH they passed through the Red Sea as by dry land: which the Egyptians assaying to do were drowned."

Moses heard and believed what God said to him, and Holy Writ places him high on the list of those who build their lives on the Rock of our salvation.

The Apostle Paul built his house upon the Rock. Stern religionist, Pharisee of the Pharisees, wholly dedicated to carry out the task of exterminating the Christians, as Saul of Tarsus he journeyed toward Damascus with papers from the religious authorities which would permit him to arrest and imprison believers—men and women. But Jesus spoke to him, called him by name, and Paul asked, "Lord, what wilt thou have me to do?" From that moment on, as Paul the Apostle, he heard and obeyed as God directed him in his ministry. Aside from the Lord Jesus Christ, I doubt that any other person suffered as much and remained as faithful as did this Hebrew of the Hebrews who *HEARD and OBEYED* the sayings of Jesus. He became the great apostle to the Gentiles, and it was to him that God revealed the mystery of the New Testament Church, the mystery hidden from all eternity (Eph. 3:1—12). Paul built on the Rock from his conversion until the day he sealed his testimony with his life's blood. Hear the words of his final testimony to young Timothy:

"I am now ready to be offered, and the time of my departure is at hand. I HAVE FOUGHT A GOOD FIGHT, I have FINISHED MY COURSE, I have KEPT THE FAITH: henceforth there is laid up for me a crown of righteousness, which the Lord, the Righteous Judge, shall give me at that day—and not to me only, but unto all them also that love His appearing" (II Tim. 4:6—8).

Now by way of contrast let us look at some of the men in Scripture who built their houses on the sand. They *HEARD* the words of Jesus, but *they did not DO them.* What about Judas Iscariot, for example?

Who ever had a greater opportunity to *HEAR and HEED* the words of Jesus? Judas was one of the twelve. He walked and talked with Jesus through most of the Lord's public ministry. He witnessed many of His great miracles, no doubt he was present when Lazarus was called forth from the grave, and he helped to serve the loaves and fishes when Jesus fed the five thousand. Times without number he heard the *wonderful words of life* spoken by Jesus, but he did not hear with his heart. He heard only with his ears, and *he did not OBEY what he heard.* He built his house on the sand, and when the floods came and the hurricanes of hell beat in upon it, it fell—and great was the fall thereof. In Luke 22:3, 4 we read, "Then entered Satan into Judas surnamed Iscariot, being of the number of the twelve. *And HE WENT HIS WAY, and communed with the chief priests and captains, how he might betray (Jesus) unto them.*"

Notice: Judas *"went his way"*—but *HIS way* was not the *Jesus way.* His way was the way of greed, gain, and personal glory. He betrayed the Lord, he collected his bargain of thirty pieces of silver—but what did it profit him? Jesus asked, "What is a man profited, if he shall gain the whole world, and lose his own soul? Or what shall a man give in exchange for his soul? For the Son of man shall come in the glory of His Father with His angels; and then He shall reward every man according to his works" (Matt. 16:26, 27).

In Matthew 27:1—8 we read of the outcome of Judas: "When the morning was come, all the chief priests and elders of the people took counsel against Jesus to put Him to death: and when they had bound Him, they led Him away, and delivered Him to Pontius Pilate the governor.

"Then JUDAS, which had betrayed Him, when he saw that He was condemned, *repented himself,* and brought again the thirty pieces of silver to the chief priests and elders, saying, I have sinned in that I have betrayed the innocent blood. And they said, What is that to us? see thou to that. *AND HE CAST DOWN THE PIECES OF SILVER IN THE TEMPLE, and DEPARTED, and WENT AND HANGED HIMSELF!*

"And the chief priests took the silver pieces, and said, It is not lawful for to put them into the treasury, because it is the price of blood. And they took counsel, and bought with them the potter's field, to bury strangers in. Wherefore that field was called, The field of blood, unto this day."

In Acts 1:18 Peter tells us that Judas "falling headlong . . . burst asunder in the midst, and all his bowels gushed out." What a contrast to the end of earthly life for the Apostle Paul, who built his spiritual life on the Rock, Christ Jesus—yet Paul was not one of the twelve, he did not see the miracles Judas saw, he did not hear the sermons of Jesus as Judas heard them. He simply heard and obeyed what Jesus said to *him.*

In Genesis chapters 6 and 7 we find the account of an entire civilization that built on sand; but the flood came, and they found their house would not stand. Only Noah and his family were saved, only Noah's house stood the storm; for it was built according to God's blueprint: *"Thus did NOAH: According to all that God commanded him, SO DID HE!"* (Gen. 6:22).

Pharaoh built his house on the sand. If you will study Exodus chapters 8 through 12 you will find that Pharaoh was warned time after time—he heard God's message through Moses and Aaron, but he did not heed it. He refused to do what God told him to do. But Moses had built on the Rock, and while he and the children of Israel crossed the Red Sea on dry land, a few minutes later *"the waters returned, and covered the chariots, and the horsemen, and all the host of Pharaoh that came into the sea after them; THERE REMAINED NOT SO MUCH AS ONE OF THEM"* (Ex. 14:28).

Nebuchadnezzar is another example of a man who built on sand—and great as his building was, when the storms came and the winds and rain beat against it, great was the fall of it! The same is true of Belshazzar, successor to Nebuchadnezzar. He defied God—he even drank wine from the gold and silver vessels which belonged in God's house. He praised the gods of silver and gold—but his house, built on sand, crumbled and fell. Read the first five chapters of Daniel for the full account of these two great kings who were foolish enough to build on sand, instead of building on the Rock, the solid Foundation.

The Jews who lived when Jesus dwelt among men heard the words of the Son of God as He spoke to the multitudes. They saw His miracles, but they refused to accept Him as Messiah, they refused to believe His sayings. His yearning over His beloved city Jerusalem is expressed in Luke 13:34, 35:

"O Jerusalem, Jerusalem, which killest the prophets, and stonest them that are sent unto thee; how often would I have gathered thy children together, as a hen doth gather her brood under her wings, AND YE WOULD NOT! Behold, your house is left unto you desolate. And verily I say unto you, Ye shall not see me, until the time come when ye shall say, Blessed is He that cometh in the name of the Lord." They HEARD—but they refused to DO; and their house built on sand fell, just as Jesus told them in Matthew 24:2 when He said to His disciples, "See ye not all these things? Verily I say unto you, There shall not be left here one stone upon another, that shall not be thrown down!" Titus the Roman fulfilled this prophecy in 70 A. D. when he leveled the city of Jerusalem and slaughtered millions of Jews. They could have built on the Rock, Christ Jesus, but they chose to build on sand.

TWIN RESULTS

"And the rain descended, and the floods came, and the winds blew, and beat upon that house;

276

and it FELL NOT: for it was founded upon a Rock. . . . And the rain descended, and the floods came, and the winds blew, and beat upon that house; and it FELL: and great was the fall of it" (Matt. 7:25, 27).

Here we see *the twin RESULTS* of building on the Rock and building on the sand. The first house stood the storm. The hurricanes of hell and the tornadoes of the damned could not destroy it. Why! Because it was FOUNDED UPON A ROCK. Nothing is said about the framing, not a word about the rafters, the roof, the floor or sub-floor. The FOUNDATION made the difference between this house and the second house, the house that fell when the storms beat upon it. The foolish builder of that house built on SAND. He might have used the very best materials, he might have hired the best contractor available; but the foundation was SAND, and sand will not, cannot, support a building.

I ask you again, dear reader: *On what are YOU building?* Are you saved—or do you just have "religion"? Like the *buildings* in our text, all of the religions on earth can be classified under two headings: The one and only true religion, CHRISTIANITY, is founded on the ROCK, Christ Jesus (Matt. 16:18). All other religions are founded on the Antichrist.

Only Christianity teaches that Christ is the ONLY way of salvation. All other religions, without exception, *add* something to Christ, or take something away. Christianity teaches that Christ is "the Author and Finisher" of our faith (Heb. 12:2), that the BLOOD of Christ is necessary—ALL that is necessary—for salvation (Col. 1:20; Heb. 9:22; I John 1:7).

Christianity teaches that believers are COMPLETE and PERFECT in Christ. Nothing can be added to perfection, nothing must be taken away. (Read Colossians 2:8—10; I Corinthians 1:30, 31; Revelation 22:18, 19.)

All religions that add to or take from the finished work of Jesus are religions built on SAND. They will not stand the tests of time or the storms of judgment. Many religions are beautiful, many are attractive to live by—but there is ONLY ONE religion that will do to DIE by, and that is CHRISTIANITY—"Christ in YOU, the hope of glory" (Col. 1:27). "If in this life only we have hope in Christ, we are of all men most miserable." So said the Apostle Paul in I Corinthians 15:19.

Beloved, if you are building on the sure foundation, the Rock, Christ Jesus, you have nothing to fear. Your house will stand the storm. But if you are building on sand, it matters not how beautiful your house may be, nor how much thought and planning you may put into it, IT WILL FALL.

If you do not *know* whether you are building on the Rock or on sand, stop right now and bow your head and talk to Jesus. Talk to Him about your soul just as you would talk to your doctor about your personal problems. If God's Spirit does not assure you that you are saved, then you are NOT SAVED! (Rom. 8:9, 14, 16; Eph. 4:30).

I John 3:19—21 tells us, "Hereby we know that we are of the TRUTH, and shall assure our hearts before Him. For if our heart condemn us, God is greater than our heart, and knoweth all things. Beloved, if our heart condemn us not, then have we confidence toward God." So have a heart-to-heart talk with yourself, and if your own heart will not give you assurance of salvation, then talk to Jesus and ask HIM for assurance.

Yes, you CAN know you are saved, just as surely as you know that you are breathing, just as surely as you know the color of your skin—or eyes, or hair. *Paul knew HE was saved* (II Tim. 1:12), and SO CAN YOU! Read the following Scriptures. Read them slowly, carefully, prayerfully—and do what they tell you to do:

John 3:16—18: "God so loved the world, that He gave His only begotten Son, that whosoever believeth in Him should not perish, but have everlasting life. For God sent not His Son into the world to condemn the world; but that the world through Him might be saved. He that believeth on Him is not condemned: but he that believeth not is condemned already, because he hath not believed in the name of the only begotten Son of God."

John 5:24: "Verily, verily, I say unto you, He that heareth my Word, and believeth on Him that sent me, hath everlasting life, and shall not come into condemnation; but is passed from death unto life."

John 14:6: "Jesus saith unto him, I am the Way, the Truth, and the Life: No man cometh unto the Father, but by me."

Acts 16:31: "Believe on the Lord Jesus Christ, and thou shalt be saved, and thy house."

Romans 10:9, 10: "If thou shalt confess with thy mouth the Lord Jesus, and shalt believe in thine heart that God hath raised Him from the dead, thou shalt be saved. For with the heart man believeth unto righteousness; and with the mouth confession is made unto salvation."

Ephesians 2:8, 9: "For by grace are ye saved through faith; and that not of yourselves: it is the gift of God: Not of works, lest any man should boast."

I John 1:9: "If we confess our sins, He is faithful and just to forgive us our sins, and to cleanse us from all unrighteousness."

NOW BOW YOUR HEAD, tell Jesus you believe what you have read, and ask Him to forgive your sins, come into your heart, and save you. He will do it—and you will know it!

NOW thank Him for saving you!